In Jeopardy

TO KNOW   TO UNDERSTAND   TO PARTICIPATE
THE CANADIAN HERITAGE IS YOUR HERITAGE

**ALBERTA HERITAGE
LEARNING RESOURCES
PROJECT**

A Project of Alberta Education
Funded
By
The Alberta Heritage Savings Trust Fund
and
Dedicated to the Students
of Alberta
by the
Government of Alberta
1979

Grateful acknowledgment is extended
to those who assisted in the development
of the Alberta Heritage anthologies

Members of the Selection Committee

Theresa Ford / *Edmonton Catholic School District*
Michael Allen / *Calgary Catholic School District*
Tom Gee / *Alberta Education*
Marg Iveson / *Edmonton Public School District*
Gloria Limin / *Calgary Public School District*
Lorne MacRae / *Calgary Public School District*
Maureen Ross / *Edmonton Catholic School District*

Western Canadian Literature
for Youth

In Jeopardy

Theresa M. Ford
Managing Editor

Alberta Education
Edmonton

Alberta Education
Devonian Building
11160 Jasper Avenue
Edmonton, Alberta
T5K 0L2

ISBN 0-920794-00-9

Project Director / Dr. Kenneth Nixon
Design / David Shaw & Associates Ltd.
Publishing Consultants / Hurtig Publishers, Edmonton
Illustration / Bill Russell
Photography / Nancy Shanoff
Typesetting / The Albertan, Calgary
Printing / Lawson Graphics Western Ltd., Calgary
Binding / Economy Bookbinding Company Ltd., Calgary

To the Reader

In Jeopardy is all about danger.

You will read about the dangers people face from their environment and from the forces of nature. They usually have very little control over the elements of fire, wind, rain, and snow, and can only react with intelligence and instinct.

You will read about the danger people face from one another in conflict situations. Many of these stories date back to events at the turn of the century. Have human emotions and motives undergone a noticeable change since that time?

You will also read about the greatest conflict of all: man *versus* himself. How do you think *you* would react in comparable situations?

No person would ever face *all* the dangers related in this book. However, while reading these accounts, be prepared to experience a tingling of the spine as though you, too, were *In Jeopardy*.

Contents

Man *vs* Himself

Brother, It's Hot

Frank W. Anderson

James Templeton undid another button at the neck of his shirt and sat up on the edge of the bed. "Brother, it's hot!" he gasped. "Reminds me of that day last winter when I was in Houston, Texas. Intense, hot, sultry. Then, bammo! A cyclone whips out of the west and I find myself flat on my back."

His roommate simply grunted, refusing to become involved in another long discussion of the Houston cyclone — he had heard the story twenty times already.

James Templeton moved to the window and looked out across the young city. From the room on the top floor of the Wascana Hotel he could see a few people on the street, but most were inside, or on front porches, trying to escape the heat. Otherwise it was a typical Sunday afternoon in the prairie metropolis of Regina, Saskatchewan.

There was a difference. The morrow would be July 1st — July 1st, 1912 — Dominion Day. Hundreds of flags and banners were flying, thousands of colored lights were strung across main thoroughfares, and seemingly miles of bunting festooned the quiet city. At that moment, the flags hung limply from their poles, the lights scarcely swayed, and the bunting looked wilted.

Suddenly, James Templeton became very attentive to a

large black cloud that hung low over the southern skyline. "Hey, Bill! Come look at this!"

There was a compelling urgency in his voice that brought his companion to his side quickly.

To the southeast of the city, a dangerous looking cloud had formed and seemed to be moving rapidly towards the west. Even as they watched, they saw a similar cloud coming in from the southwest. Within the space of moments, the two ominous-looking clouds touched hands.

"It's a cyclone," Templeton whispered in awe. "It's just like some fabled giant!!"

As they watched, they saw a dark, sinister funnel stab earthward; they thought they could hear an awful roar — even though the clouds had joined at least ten miles south of them; then they thought they could detect a rapid movement of the storm towards the city. They waited no longer. With the cyclone-experienced James Templeton in the lead, they headed for the basement of their hotel.

At the Mounted Police barracks 2½ miles west of the city, Inspector Burnett, Veterinary Surgeon, stood looking out in the direction of the city. The day, like the three which had preceded it, was exceptionally hot, even for the sun-baked prairie community. Some called the heat "unprecedented".

The flag in the barracks square, which had been stirring, fell still. A short calm followed and then abruptly the flag began to flutter briskly. At this moment, the inspector noticed "It".

It was "a great brown cloud, about two or three miles south of the city. This cloud had a peculiar edging of black and suddenly as we watched it, it appeared to form a wedge shape and rush towards the city at a tremendous pace. It was possible, even at that distance, to hear the noise. It can best be explained," Burnett recalled later, "as that of a heavy freight train crossing over a bridge."

Nevertheless, there was no alarm. A heavy rain began to fall and the downpour lasted some 20 minutes. During this time, Inspector Burnett tried to phone the Sergeant on duty in the town picket office in Regina, but the line was evidently down.

Mrs. Harry R. Belt, wife of the manager of the Merchant's Bank of Regina, who was sitting on the porch of her home at 2163 Lorne Street, noticed the great dark cloud forming in the south. She remarked on it to Mrs. John Nichol, wife of the postmaster, whose house and porch adjoined theirs. However, it merely looked like the beginning of a severe electrical storm.

"We will have to get inside soon," someone said.

Hardly were these words spoken than the wind quickened and a few preliminary drops of rain fell. The Belt family picked up their rugs and chairs and moved inside.

All along Lorne Street, other refugees from the heat began to rise leisurely and to move inside, pleased that the promise of rain would finally break the four-day heat wave.

Over on Smith Street, a block to the west, young Arthur Donaldson, carpenter, moved leisurely along the street in the general direction of the YMCA where he was staying. He was in no hurry. It was too hot to hurry. Even his brown mongrel dog, a faithful companion who accompanied him everywhere he went, was too busy panting to bother investigating the trees invitingly close.

As the wind became brisker and light rain began to fall gently, Donaldson quickened his pace.

Vincent H. Smith slumped on the bench at the boat house at Wascana Park, and stared morosely at his shoe tips. He had the strangest feeling — almost a premonition that something terrible was going to happen. He had expressed this foreboding to his friend, E. O. Gimson, as early as the previous evening, and it had been with great reluctance that he had agreed to accompany Gimson for a boat outing on the city's popular Wascana Lake.

Gimson watched him. It wasn't normal for the popular young real-estate salesman to be so gloomy. A former mayor of Balgonie, a thriving town 15 miles east of Regina, Vincent was known for his light-hearted approach to life. All in all, with Vincent's glum moping, it had been a dismal afternoon of boating and the pair had left the lake fifteen minutes ago.

Suddenly, there was a gust of wind which blew open the boat house door. Both Smith and Gimson jumped up and slammed it shut. Both saw that the sky to the south, directly over the Legislative Buildings across the lake, was dark and threatening.

Eleven-year-old Bruce Langton and his pal, Philip Steele, also eleven, saw the storm coming, but with the reckless bravado of youth decided to ignore it. Then they became aware that all around them other canoes, boats and even the sailing vessels, were racing for shore. Catching a scent of danger, they bent their backs and began to paddle for dear life — but they had such a long way to go . . .

Alex Rowbotham stood in the pergola that overlooked the beach at Wascana Park and watched the canoes and boats skipping towards shore. His eyes searched anxiously for his three friends who had gone swimming. Beside him on the wooden bench that ran around the inside of the little latticed structure were three piles of clothing — watches and valuables safely tucked in pants' pockets.

Demon Of Destruction

Like two conspirators of evil who sensed a kindred soul in each other, the two ill-omened clouds dashed across the southern sky

— met and embraced — and from their union a dark funnel of destruction leaped earthward and touched the ground about 3 miles southwest of the present junction of the Trans-Canada Highway. At the tip of the funnel, which licked angrily at the bare prairie, a tremendous rotary action developed.

Like most North American tornadoes this one was about 300-400 yards in width at the base and moved from southwest to northwest at speeds varying from 10 to 50 miles per hour. Its rotation was counter-clockwise and the speed of the winds around the vortex (or the "eye") were probably between 100 and 500 miles per hour. Within the "eye" or vortex was a very low barometric pressure caused by the centrifugal effect of the winds — creating almost a vacuum-like effect. As the tail of the twister touched the ground it caught up dirt and debris, causing the bottom part of the tornado to appear dark brown.

The vicious tail of the tornado touched the farm buildings of Thomas Beare, about 11 miles southwest of the city. It pushed them over like pasteboards, tossing lumber, farm machinery and animals around like toothpicks.

Leaving the Beare family bruised and battered from flying debris, the tornado began to race across the prairie, wreaking death and destruction as it charged senselessly ahead. Two miles north, it licked at the farm of Walter Stephenson, a young farmer just out from Pickering County, near Whitby, Ontario. Plucking the house from above their heads, the swirling funnel slammed Stephenson against the crumpled lumber and snatched up his young bride of three months and hurled her a hundred yards across the farmyard. It stripped her practically naked — even the shoes were wrenched from her feet — before it left her bruised and bleeding from numerous tiny cuts.

Almost as if sensing that bigger prey lay ahead, the malefic funnel suddenly swung northward towards the city of 10,000. On its way, it paused to drop in on the Dunlops. Like their neighbors, the Dunlops were from Ontario and were newly married — having taken the fatal step only the Christmas before. Demolishing the house and barn, the tornado severely injured both the newly-weds as it swept towards an unsuspecting Regina.

Directly across the road from the Dunlop farm was the home of Robert Kerr. The lashing tail flicked at the buildings, pulverizing them. It killed Andrew Roy, of Horwick, Quebec, who was visiting at the farmhouse; cut both Mr. and Mrs. Kerr with flying glass; and broke the arm of their eight-year-old daughter.

A quarter mile down the road, it sideswiped the Calvin Presbyterian Church, literally tearing it apart.

Moving with what was then incredible speed, the tornado roared towards Regina. The Mooney farm, rented by an Old Country couple named James, was lashed into shapelessness in seconds. Mr. John James, his wife Maud, their child Amy and their hired man were left broken and wounded. All required prolonged treatment in hospital.

Then, almost as if momentarily sated with its initial taste of blood, the gigantic whirlwind veered away from the homes of Thomas Elliott and his brother, James. It levelled both their dairy barns and strewed bawling cattle about like toys, but left their houses intact.

Directly ahead of the Elliott farms lay the Legislative Buildings. To the right was the city power plant, with its tall smokestack jutting into the sky, and north of the power plant was the Provincial Jail. Providentially the storm followed a path that missed all of them.

Sweeping between the Legislative Buildings and the power plant, the tornado reached out with gigantic, powerful fingers of wind and suction and smashed the windows of the Legislature. Partitions inside were ripped out indiscriminately and furniture overturned. Prankishly the wind flicked at a table in the Department of Education on which were piled the examination papers for all Saskatchewan Grade Schools and flung them far and wide. As a result, teachers across the province had to pass, or fail, their pupils on their recollection of the year's work.

Then the tornado leaped upon the peaceful waters of Wascana Lake.

Death Dance at Wascana

Alex Rowbotham, who was guarding the valuables and clothing of his friends in the pergola at Wascana, was probably the first person to realize the danger to the infant city as the giant twister came roaring around the majestic Legislative Buildings and ripped up the lake, but if he did, it was a momentary, fleeting realization. Stunned, he watched it careen towards him, lifting a gigantic spout of water into its vortex. He was aware that the roof had gone from over his head and that one of the walls was falling towards him . . .

He awoke in the hospital.

Bruce Langton and Philip Steele were nearly to shore when the water heaved under them, lifting their canoe bodily out of the water and twirling it. Young Steele was instantly killed as he was flung from the canoe to the grass, but Bruce Langton, unconscious, rode the crazily spinning canoe deep into Wascana Park.

Freakishly, the whirling wind deposited the boat right side up near 16th Avenue (now College). It was said by rescuers that Bruce still had a paddle clutched in his hands when they found him, dazed and shaken, sitting bolt upright in the canoe.

Two days later, he was still too unnerved to even remember the name of his dead chum!

Light canoes, sailing vessels and some dinghies were plucked up like matches and tossed crazily through the air. Parts of canoes landed in Victoria Park, half a mile distant. One fragment even sailed through the fourth floor window of the Kerr Building, where Mr. Soskin, director of the local Film

Exchange, had barricaded himself. The piece of canoe narrowly missed Soskin as it crashed against the opposite wall of the room.

In the boat house at Wascana, about a dozen young sailing devotees had taken shelter from the anticipated rain storm. At first they treated the storm with supreme contempt — as befitted good inland sailors — but as the wind increased in ferocity they began to realize that this was no ordinary rain. A sudden gust of wind blew open the door and Vincent H. Smith and his friend E. O. Gimson leaped to close it. There was a momentary lull and then, with an ear-deafening roar, the door flew off its hinges and the whole building shook and fell apart.

Ten-year-old Leonard Marshall, who had just finished a swim, was still struggling into his shirt in the boathouse when he was picked up bodily and hurled through the air. The next thing he knew he was lying on wet grass about 150 yards away. Surprised, a bit bruised, but relatively unharmed, he jumped to his feet. The following wind caught him and pushed him ahead of it, while torrents of water, scooped from the lake, swirled around him. He ran.

He ran and he ran ahead of the wind, almost oblivious to the incredible scenes of destruction around him. He had reached Victoria Park, half a mile away, before he fell to the ground — exhausted.

An unknown passerby found him lying there — beside the fragments of a canoe — and picked him up in his arms and carried him into a nearby house to be cared for.

Hardly a man in the boathouse was unscathed as the structure was completely demolished. Some, like Albert Ehlside, of 1734 Lorne Street, escaped with minor injuries and immediately ran for their homes — fearful of what they might find. Others, like E. O. Gimson, whose feet were painfully crushed, dragged themselves out of the ruins, or picked themselves up from the grass where they had been dropped by the demonic winds, and went in search of friends.

Albert Ehlside was lucky. He arrived home to find his

house in ruins, but his widowed mother safe — sitting disconsolately on a box near what had been her home.

E. O. Gimson was not lucky. "The second and more violent gust of wind carried the door off its hinges," Mr. Gimson told reporters from his hospital bed two days later. "That was the last I saw of Vincent Smith. The next thing I remember is waking up in the park. So I must have been blown up over the bank. We searched for Vincent nearly all night and I must have walked miles during that time. I did not notice any pain at that time."

They found Vincent H. Smith in a pile of rubble on Smith Street, to which the force of the wind had rolled, tumbled and tossed him. He was dead — battered almost beyond recognition.

Doctors who examined Mr. Gimson said that it was incredible that he had walked a foot and that it would be weeks before his crushed feet would heal sufficiently to bear his weight.

In the terrifying confusion that followed the striking of the tornado, it was inevitable that many rumors would begin. An early report that gained wide circulation was that "at least five people were drowned in a monstrous water spout at Wascana Lake." This report seemed to gain body and credence when Mr. Alex Rowbotham reported that his three friends had not come out of the water to claim their clothing in the pergola before he and it were blown away. He was positive that they had been drowned — otherwise they would have come to see him.

A day after Mr. Rowbotham circulated his story, his three companions were located. Two had been seriously injured and the other was unharmed. All three had actually left the water and were walking towards the pergola when the cyclone hit it. Mr. Rowbotham had evidently been so petrified by the terrible sight of the tornado bearing down upon him that he had not seen them.

Those who viewed the carnage at Wascana Lake — the wreckage of the boat house, the swimming house, the Heman boat livery and the pergola, the broken boats strewn far and wide — were ready to believe any story, no matter how fantastic.

One of the fantastic stories — totally without any foundation — concerned the canoe which hit the Kerr building. Later reports by news-hungry story tellers embellished this fact by claiming that Vincent H. Smith was actually in the canoe when it crashed through the fourth floor window!

The reporters who swarmed through the ruins for days to come, interviewed everyone who wasn't too busy repairing bodies or houses to talk. Somewhere along the route a reporter interviewed the unknown man who had found Leonard Marshall lying in Victoria Park near the ruins of a canoe. The reporter connected the two — the boy and the canoe — and newspapers across the country picked up the story of Leonard Marshall and his wild ride from Wascana Lake to Victoria Park astride a canoe! It was a beautiful story — it had color, it was fantastic, and it was utterly believable.

Leonard's mother, who with typical maternal concern noticed that her son was incredibly dirty when they brought him home, later tried to discredit the story, but without success. Somehow over the years stories of Bruce Langton and Leonard Marshall have become entangled into one fable — and the legend now seems to get better with each resurrection.

Because of the persistent rumors of wholesale drownings at Wascana, there was even talk of draining the lake to search for victims, or of using dynamite to bring bodies to the surface, but, as the list of missing persons dwindled and finally vanished, it became evident that only young Philip Arthur Steele and Vincent H. Smith had lost their lives at Wascana.

Blood, Death and Laughter

As Mr. and Mrs. Belt, of 2163 Lorne Street, picked up their rugs and chairs and carried them inside in preparation for the coming "electrical storm", Mr. Belt climbed the stairs automatically to shut the bedroom windows. Before he got there, there was a crash and the windows disappeared. Mrs. Belt rushed to close the front door, but it was gone. Alarmed, she caught her two children by the hand and literally dragged them into the cellar. A white faced Mr. Belt tumbled in beside them.

"The roof at the back of the house was blown off," said Mrs. Belt, "and we looked up at the open sky. Everything in the cellar was swimming round and round in a wild circuit, and as we looked at the walls, it seemed only to need another blow and they would fall. Then there came a terrific roar. It took up everything that was in the way. It shot something hard right through the walls of the house.

"We stood there, crouching for a time, scared as could be. There was no thought of tears. It had been but a few moments, but it seemed like a lifetime. Then the rain came like a deluge and soaked everything in the house which was exposed to the storm.

"Later, when the fury seemed to have subsided, we crept around — almost sneaking you might say — and peered out the window. Why, where is the brick house on the corner, we asked ourselves? It was gone. Not one brick was left on top of the other. We thought the storm had only hit us, but as we looked around . . . we got a glimpse of the terrible sight of havoc all around us."

This experience was repeated over and over again in the sprawling prairie metropolis of Regina that grim afternoon of Sunday, June 30th, 1912, as the demonic, lashing tail of the tornado cut a swath of death and destruction through the very heart of the city. Sometimes there was a happy ending, as with the Belts, but all too frequently the ending was bloody and tragic.

Like the Belts, few realized the extent of the catastrophe until they had shaken themselves free of their own personal wreckage and had walked about on the streets. Many thought "the storm had hit only us." Others, just outside the disaster area, were incredulous when they discovered what had actually happened. Several recalled that they had laughed at the spectacle of a man running down McIntyre Street being chased by a barrel. Others had been highly amused at the antics of the wind as it tossed papers and litter through the air. Many, on the fringes of the blast, were frightened. Only as the city dwellers began to clear away the wreckage did they begin to appreciate both the magnitude of the calamity and the protectiveness of the hand of Fate that seemed to have ridden with the storm.

The tornado struck on Sunday afternoon at 4:50 p.m. It caught a city resting, seeking shelter from the oppressive heat. It caught schools emptied for the first day of summer holidays; it caught the business section almost deserted; it caught the churches between morning and evening congregations; it caught empty houses whose occupants were visiting in other, untouched areas of the city. It struck a city leisurely waiting to enjoy the Dominion Day celebrations ahead; a city of hundreds of flags and banners; a city of a thousand strings of colored lights strung from lamppole to lamppole.

Another incredible feature of the punishing funnel of fury was that — after a relatively wide swath on the prairie — the lashing tail of the tornado seems to have steadied down and to have sliced a narrow path through the city at right angles. Not until it reached the CPR tracks and the warehouse district did the storm splay out again. Beyond the tracks, on the North Side, it fanned out, engulfing a wider area as it laid waste the flimsy wooden structures and then lost itself and its fury on the open prairies beyond.

This fortuitous circumstance undoubtedly reduced the amount of damage and confined the eventual death toll.

Path of Destruction

With three victims to its credit before it even reached the densely populated residential area of the city, the tornado pounced upon the unprepared city and began its grim, freakish game of hit and miss.

Probably no one will ever know how long the reign of terror hung over the prairie oasis of Regina. Some estimates say it was all over in 30 seconds. More probably the raging twister took as long as four or even five minutes to traverse the city. Preceded by a very light rain, the main body of the storm was followed by a deluge of water — some of it sucked up from Wascana and dumped upon the nearest buildings as if from a giant pail. With the cessation of the torrential downpour, people began to crawl from the ruins of their homes, or to venture from the safety of buildings untouched by the tornado, and to form rescue parties.

One of the first homes struck was that of William Beelby. Beelby, a stone mason, who lived at 2354 Smith Street, was resting in the upper bedroom of his two storey house, together with his wife and his 3-year-old daughter, Florence. The entire top floor was cut loose from the house, carried across the street and deposited on a neighbor's front lawn. Scarcely scratched, Mr. and Mrs. Beelby crawled through a broken window. They immediately discovered that the baby was missing, and despite the drenching downpour, began to hunt for her. When eventually found, tiny Florence Beelby was in the oven of the cookstove in the middle of the street. Her face was badly bruised and her ankle black and blue. It is probable that Florence, thrown out of the house, had crawled inside the oven for protection from the rain.

The first to die was young Fred Hindson, of 2220 Lorne Street. Fred had just graduated from the School of Pharmacy at the University of Toronto and was then working as a clerk in the local post-office. His father, James Hindson, tells the story graphically. "When I first realized the enormous proportions of the storm about to strike us, I called to the children to run to the cellar. I also shouted for Mrs. Hindson and Bob Edgar, who were in the front of the house on the ground floor, but apparently they did not hear me. Fred, Douglas and myself were in the entrance to the cellar when the full force of the storm hit the house and it immediately crumbled. Fred, my son, was probably hit with something and killed outright. He was thrown to the floor and I was also thrown in such a position that my hand was stretched over his body. He was lying still and I instantly felt he was dead."

Douglas Hindson, 15, was "struck with something behind the ear and all scratched up considerably", but managed to wiggle loose and climb from the wreckage. He ran for help and returned with a neighbor, John Gardner.

The rescuers, led by John Gardner, were stunned at the extent of the damage, but pitched in. In the ruins they could hear the cries of the nine persons injured and trapped, and while they worked as rapidly as they could, it was slow progress to reach them. Every time they moved a timber, they were afraid they would kill some of those pinned underneath. "It was a scene I will never forget," said Gardner.

They found Fred Hindson dead and his father so badly battered that he was thought also to be dead. In fact, his name even appeared as a casualty on the initial lists of dead. Not one of the nine persons escaped injury. Improvised ambulances rushed them to the General Hospital — which was already filling up with wounded.

Next door to the Hindson residence, rescuers dug frantically through the rubble to locate Albert G. Weeks, of 2216 Lorne Street. When they found him, they first believed him to be dead, but a faint heart beat was present and he was rushed to hospital. He lingered near death through the night, but by Monday evening he began to recover from the devastating blow he had received.

Not so lucky were the residents of Joseph Jack's rooming house next door at 2202 Lorne.

"I was in my room when the house first began to rock, reminding me of a ship at sea," said Kenneth Reid, of Trenton, Ohio. "Then it started to twirl round and round and I was hurled from wall to wall."

Reid escaped with minor cuts and bruises, but Andrew Boyd, a retired farmer from Sherwood, who was boarding at the Jack home, was taken from the ruins seriously injured. Rushed to General Hospital, the oldster lingered for two days before succumbing to his wounds.

James Patrick Coffee, a native of Lisbon, Ireland, was taken from the rubble . . . dead.

Mrs. Jack, formerly of Calgary, Alberta, was thought to be dying from a massive blow to the back of her head, but an emergency trepanation was performed at the General and her life was saved.

There was one solid block of residences between Lorne and Smith Streets and bounded by 13th and 14th Avenues which was levelled. Caught squarely in the heart of the tornado, many of them were battered down by the rotary force of the winds. Others literally blew themselves up as the low-pressure area of the tornado passed over them. The air remaining inside the house created an outward pressure and when the core of the storm reached them, creating almost a vacuum, this inside pressure burst the walls, thrust up the ceiling and shredded doors and windows. The devastation in this one block was almost complete, yet, strangely enough there was only one death amid this wreckage. Donald Miller Loggie, infant son of Mr. and Mrs. Harold N. Loggie, of 2201 Smith Street, was instantly killed by the bursting of their home.

Half a block west of the Loggie home, the tornado demolished the grocery and meat store of Paul McElmoyle at 2318 — 15th Avenue. At the approach of the storm, Mr. McElmoyle began to herd his three small children down from the living quarters above the store to the cellar. "With my wife, I was within one second of being safely in the cellar," he said later. "I was horrified to see my wife fall, struck by something, and myself rendered helpless to assist her by the debris piled around me. It is a very hard loss to bear with three small, motherless children." Mrs. McElmoyle was victim No. 8.

Leaving broken homes, broken bones and bodies in its wake, the tornado swept on towards the business section of Regina. The Guthrie home, 2138 Lorne Street, was a little cottage nestled between two sturdier houses. Owned by Mrs. M. A. Guthrie, widow of J. Guthrie, it served as home for her three grown daughters, Etta, Mary and Violet. Mr. F. W. Harris, an accountant for Reeves & Co., and his wife also roomed there.

When rescuers reached the building, they found Etta Guthrie, the eldest daughter, dead. There was an engagement ring on her finger and it is said that her fiance had himself miraculously escaped from the flattened cottage. He was found, dazed and bleeding, sitting in the ruins.

Mrs. Harris "was carried out of the ruins a terrible sight. She was literally smashed to a pulp. She had evidently been caught in a mass of timbers and crushed." Taken to hospital, Mrs. Harris lingered for a short while before death came to her.

No one in the house escaped serious injury. Mr. Harris was taken from the wreck and carried to the Roman Catholic Bishop's Palace on McIntyre Street, which while badly damaged, was still usable. Like many another person who was carried into a nearby building for care and shelter, Mr. Harris was believed to be dead or missing when the first count of casualties was taken. However, Mr. Harris recovered sufficiently to accompany the remains of his wife to Brandon, Manitoba, for burial two days later.

Unsated in its senseless destruction, the tornado swept down upon Mack Lee's Chinese laundry, demolishing it with a wisp of effort. Mr. Alex Huston, of the Municipal Department, who was one of the first rescuers on the scene of the destroyed laundry on the corner of Smith and 13th, found one Chinese, Ywe Boyuen, still trapped under the building. The other Chinese occupants refused to touch Ywe, saying that he was dead and that they could not touch a dead man. Believing that the man was still alive, Mr. Huston organized a rescue squad from passers-by and attempted to free the aged Chinese. As they worked frantically they could see that he was still alive, but before they could reach him he succumbed. He was taken to nearby Speers Undertaking Parlors.

With 11 victims to its credit, the merciless storm blundered on.

The home of J. E. Price at 2069 Lorne Street was completely overturned, and was hurtled on top of the cottage of H. L. Potts next door. The only part of Mr. Potts' house that remained after the storm was the rear kitchen and, miraculously, this was the spot to which Potts rushed for safety with his wife and small child. "When the storm hit us," said Mr. Potts, "I rushed for the back kitchen, hoping to get into the cellar beneath. I was halfway downstairs when the Price house landed on top of ours. I was thrown against the wall, but wiggled out. Mrs. Potts is suffering badly from shock, but neither she or the baby are injured." The only piece of furniture still intact was the piano stool.

The story is told that the next morning Mr. Potts was discovered sitting on the piano stool at the ruins of his home, reading a book. "Here is a strange coincidence," Mr. Potts remarked. "I found this book blown into my yard and it is entitled *Business Hints For The Beginner.*"

The greatest loss of life was at the Hodsman home at 1947 Smith Street. Like many another householder, Mr. James Hodsman had roomers. In this instance it was Mrs. Isabelle McKay, a widow with a 3-year-old son, Charles; and her sister, Mrs. James McKay, who worked as a maid in a local hotel to support the family. There were eight persons in the house when it came crashing down around their heads.

"When it crashed down," said Mrs. Hodsman from her hospital bed later, "Mr. Hodsman was carried right from the top floor downstairs and he didn't even get a scratch. I am so glad he is able now to look after the rest of us."

As rescuers worked through the drizzling rain which followed the tornado, they found young Mrs. McKay and her 3-year-old son dead. Lawrence Hodsman, variously described as 10 or 15 years of age, was also dead. The rest of the inmates were all seriously wounded and required hospitalization — with the exception of Mr. Hodsman.

A fourth body was found under the wreckage piled around the front porch. It was identified as that of Arthur Donaldson, the young contractor. It was not known how he arrived there until Miss McIntyre, whose house next door was also destroyed, reported that she had been looking out her front window just before the tornado struck and had seen Mr. Donaldson, accompanied by his dog, come running down the street. Donaldson had run up onto the porch of the Hodsman home, only to be crushed by the collapse of the front wall. The little brown dog had been swept on past by the winds.

During the rescue, the brown mongrel appeared at the ruined house and sat waiting. When Donaldson's body was removed to Speers Funeral Parlors, the dog tagged along. From Sunday evening until Wednesday, when Donaldson was buried, the dog kept vigil — refusing to be sent away. Then he disappeared.

Approximately one minute after leaving Wascana Lake, the "eye" of the tornado reached the business section of the city — clustered around the beautiful Victoria Park.

One of the first large buildings hit was the Land Titles Office but here the blow was glancing and relatively little damage resulted. The Metropolitan Methodist Church, one of the most magnificent edifices in the city, was directly in the heart of the twister and was destroyed.

"I was in the club room at the rear of the church when the storm broke," said Matthew Henderson. "I ran to leave the building when I saw bricks flying through the air, through the door and windows. Then I ran back to see if anyone was in the main body of the church. No one was there. I started madly to the Sunday School room, it was empty. The noise was absolutely deafening. The whole church rocked and it seemed as if the world was coming to an end. I ran back to the rear entrance and attempted to open the door. The wind was blowing so strongly, I hesitated with it partly open. Placing my knee against the door, I stood a fraction of a second. The whole side of the church collapsed and fell in front of me, brushing me by a hair's breadth with a mass of stone, brick and timber. I then crawled out over the door that acted as a shield over the ruins of the church."

Next door, the handsome YWCA building which had been completed only that spring, caught the full brunt of the storm. Miss Ella Bowers and a friend, Miss Donaldson, had just come in for afternoon tea and were hanging up their hats and cloaks in the lobby when bricks began hurtling down through the skylight on top of them. By a miracle, both their lives were saved, and the only serious damage was a bruised arm and crushed thumb when a door fell on Miss Bowers.

The Methodist parsonage next to the public library was laid waste. Rev. J. Lewis, whose wife was bed-ridden, rushed into the sun room over the front porch where she was lying and carried her out just as the room collapsed. He carried her in his arms to the rear entrance with dust, furniture and wood whirling around him, but found this blocked. He then made his way back to the front, but finding this stopped up by fallen stone, sat down on the stairs, holding Mrs. Lewis in his arms. They both expected instant death, but incredibly they were unmarked when rescuers dug them out.

Two bodies were found between the Methodist parsonage and the Public Library.

Frank and Bertha Blenkhorn had been visiting friends that

Sunday afternoon, and with the approach of the storm had hastily bade their hosts goodbye and had started across Victoria Park to their home at 1957 Smith Street adjacent to the ill-fated Hodsman house.

The Blenkhorns had, up to this point, borne charmed lives. Married in England in early April of that year, they had booked passage on the maiden voyage of the luxury liner the *Titanic,* but the wedding party had delayed them and they had arrived at the dock to discover that they had missed their boat. They learned later that the *Titanic* had gone to the bottom on the night of April 14-15, 1912 with a terrible loss of life.

Catching a later boat, Frank Blenkhorn had arrived in Regina late in April with his wife and after taking a temporary position as advertising solicitor for the *Daily Standard* newspaper, he had found himself caught up in the land-boom fever of the day and had gone into partnership with Alfred Boyes as the real-estate firm of Blenkhorn & Boyes.

Cutting diagonally across the beautiful Victoria Park, the Blenkhorns were somewhere in the middle of it when the full fury of the tornado struck them. Trees, so carefully planted scarcely four years before, were stripped of bark. Flower beds were whisked away and the expanses of green grass were littered and bruised by falling debris. Even the ornate fountain in the middle of the park was devastated. The Blenkhorns, caught in the open, were snatched up, twirled and tossed over and over and finally were dashed against the brick wall of the Public Library. The front wall of the Methodist parsonage next door collapsed over their prostrate bodies, burying them.

Fate, in the form of the Regina Tornado, had caught up with the charmed Blenkhorns who had come 8,000 miles to die.

The death-dealing storm paused a moment on the north side of the Park to snuff out the life of Mrs. Mary Shaw, of 2320 — 12th Avenue. Mary, wife of Samuel D. Shaw, a yardman for the CPR, was taken from the Park to the General Hospital where she died from her injuries shortly after admittance. She was the 18th sacrifice to the seemingly insatiable greed of the demonic winds.

Then it flung itself upon the stately Knox Presbyterian Church and the local YMCA.

There was fortunately no one in Knox Presbyterian Church when the blast struck, but the building itself suffered such destruction that it had to be rebuilt from the ground up.

At the YMCA, Mr. T. P. Williams and his fellow roommate G. Tierman, were lying on their beds in Room 12, trying to find surcease from the oppressive heat. "I was awakened by rain on our windows," Williams related from his hospital bed the next day. "It was so terrifying we both jumped up in our beds. I was looking over the buildings and saw debris flying. We fled to our feet and made a rush to gain the lower floor. We had hardly reached the entrance when the building shook like a leaf and appeared to crumble over our heads."

The next thing Mr. Williams remembered was awakening to find himself and his companion pinned under a mass of rubble, far from the YMCA. A large timber was bent like a match above them, supporting the weight of a brick wall which had toppled over on top of them.

After fifteen minutes, they were released from their impromptu shelter. Mr. Williams, who was not badly injured, was taken to the General Hospital, while his friend, Tierman, unharmed, enrolled in the rescue work at once.

In the Telephone Exchange Building about one block north of the YMCA, 8 operators under Chief Operator Miss Lobsinger were on duty that afternoon. A service man and a janitor were somewhere about in the building.

The tornado wreaked terrible damage on the building, tearing the roof loose and caving in the south wall. The massive switchboard, estimated to weigh some 15 tons, crashed through the floor into the basement, carrying three operators down with it still in their chairs and with their headphones still over their ears. The rest of the girls were trapped in the basement under the collapsed roof and walls, but the three operators who came down with the switchboard managed to work their way out through a basement window with the help of the janitor. They made their way to the nearby *Leader* newspaper office.

At first their story was treated with jocular good humor and they were kidded about "trying to get their names in the paper", but when the staff realized that the girls were serious they formed a rescue party and hurried to the telephone building. It was only then that they began to realize the enormous force of the storm.

In the utter confusion and lack of communication that followed immediately upon the storm, it was reported that Operator Miss Black had her back broken and was dying and that Miss Russell also had a broken back. Later, it was learned that Miss Black had not even been in the building that day and was unscathed. Miss Russell's injuries proved to be minor in nature. Though all nine girls and both men in the exhange were badly shaken up and suffered minor wounds, none was killed.

As it approached the CPR main line — along which the majority of the warehouse buildings fronted — the tornado struck five times with lightning rapidity.

At the Donaghue Block, a steel frame building which caught the full blast and stood against it, the tornado reached deadly fingers through the broken windows and snuffed the life from James Milton Scott. Ironically, Scott, a young clerk in the Customs Department, had been living at Room 104 of the New Armour Block — which escaped serious damage in the storm — and had moved to the Donaghue Block only a few days before.

At 1821 Cornwall Street, the Mah Chang Sing Laundry was instantly pulverized. Inside, Ye Wing, Charlie Sand, and their brother Chan Sun were trapped. Charlie Sand was dead when rescuers eventually reached them late that night; Ye Wing lingered over the night at the General Hospital before he joined his brother in death; and only Chan Sun survived the terrible ordeal.

On the edge of the tracks, on South Railway Street, the tornado struck the warehouse district in full flight. Already it was beginning to fan out after having pursued a relatively straight and narrow course through the residential and business areas. The Palace Livery, owned by Mr. W. H. Mulligan, was directly in the path of the storm.

The whirling blast of wind which preceded the "eye" of the tornado picked up a small boy — name unknown — and literally tossed him into the arm of Mr. Mulligan. Mr. Mulligan held the boy tightly in his arms while he, his son and the hired men who were feeding the 50 head of horses, crawled from the wrecked portion of the barn to an undamaged area. But, scarcely had they arrived at what they felt was safety, than both walls of the brick Marshall-Boyd block beside them caved in on top of the livery stable. Robert Fenwick, a young man from Smith Falls, Ontario, was instantly killed and buried beneath the tangled mass of timbers and brick.

A second later directly across the street, the tornado crushed the warehouse of Tudhope Anderson.

Mr. Joseph J. Bryan, manager of the Regina branch of the firm, was in consultation with salesman S. Ingram as the storm descended. When he was released from the mess, Ingram told rescuers: "We were in the office and could see that an extra heavy storm was coming on, but almost before we could think, we were under this pile of wreckage. Mr. Bryan, who was near me, was thrown fairly on my back as we fell to the floor. Strange to say, as we fell, I could feel his body. I called to him, but received no reply and reaching up again could feel his arm. The body became quite limp and I was quite sure he must have been killed."

Mr. Ingram lay for four hours with the dead body of his employer above him before rescuers reached him and pulled him free.

After crossing the tracks and creating havoc with the enormous grain elevators and the freight cars, all of which were tossed about with seemingly equal ease, the base of the storm broadened — almost as if it wanted to do as much damage as possible before it reached the open prairie beyond the cemetery on the north.

The "North Side" of the tracks was composed chiefly of wooden houses set apart from each other with little shelter. Many were mere shacks occupied by the poorer element of the prosperous young city. Some of the buildings — such as the Ackerman Building and the CPR roundhouse — were of substantial stone and brick. It seemed to make no difference. The force of the tornado was still powerful enough to wreck whatever it touched.

George B. Craven, a dairy instructor, aged about 35, and a former native of New Zealand, was later found near the CPR roundhouse. He had been crushed by a hurtling boxcar. Another man, William Bradshaw, a CPR checker, who was last seen in the yards near George Craven, was missing and at first believed to be dead. However, he later turned up safe at the home of a friend where he had sought help and shelter.

Beyond the CPR yards were row upon row of flimsily constructed wooden houses just on the north edge of town. One of the first victims here was Mrs. Laura McDonald, of 1438 Lorne Street North. Alarmed by the nature of the on-coming storm, but scarcely realizing its dreadful power, Mrs. McDonald had gone into the backyard to close the chicken coop securely when she was felled and killed by a flying scantling.

Almost directly across the street, at 1435 Lorne, was the rented home of James McDougall. Mr. McDougall, about 40, was a machinist for the Cockshutt Plow Co. Previous to this he had been unemployed for some time and his family — composed of himself, his wife, 4 girls and 4 boys — were having a difficult time financially. Their total worldly wealth was wrapped up in the furnishings of their rented home.

Alarmed by the awesome sight of the approaching tornado, Mrs. McDougall snatched up the youngest child — 3-year-old

Ida — and started to run outside. The side of the house fell on her as she was going through the door and she was pinned under the timbers. Inside the house, the other members of the McDougall family found themselves trapped beneath a jumble of rafters and beams.

When a rescue team finally began to remove the debris from around them, it found Mr. McDougall and his little daughter Ida in critical condition. Rushed to the Grey Nuns Hospital — the General being already filled to overflowing — Mr. McDougall died that night. Little Ida lingered for two days before finally succumbing to her injuries. Mrs. McDougall and the three daughters — Gibra, Marvel and Barbara — were placed on the critical list and it was thought that all four would die. However, they all finally recovered, though it was some time before hospital authorities dared tell Mrs. McDougall that her husband and youngest child had been killed. The four boys survived with minor scratches and were cared for at the home of a motherly neighbor — Mrs. Cameron.

The 28th and last victim of the tornado was George Appleby.

George Appleby, a young Englishman, had immigrated to Canada some three years previously and had taken up a homestead in the Swift Current district. Like many another young man of his day, he worked his homestead in the spring and fall, turning to other forms of work in the off seasons in order to survive. One of the most popular young men in the community, he was Scout Master for the Second Troop and was in charge of First Aid Work for all troops in the city.

Appleby was in a tent at the back of a house on Cornwall Street, between 7th and 8th Avenues, and evidently gauging the intensity of the storm correctly, began to run for the shelter of the house. The terrible tornado overtook him just as he got to its side. The building seemed to explode from within and one wall fell outwards upon him.

Leaving its last victim dead amid the ruins, the tornado spread out across the prairie and eventually expended itself there without further serious damage to property or human beings. Though later reports indicated that damage had been effected at least 8 miles northeast of the city — towards Balgonie — none of this damage was comparable to the havoc wrought in the prairie capitol.

The Aftermath

At 4:55 p.m. the whistle on the powerhouse blasted a belated warning to the residents of Regina. By then, the damage had been done. Twenty-eight persons were dead, or dying; hundreds were injured — some seriously, some slightly; the unharmed were beginning to venture out into the rain-drenched, litter strewn street to gaze in awe upon the dreadful scene of carnage. Then came the realization that many must still be trapped beneath the tumbled houses, the twisted masses of lumber, brick and stone. Dazed, shocked by the extent of the disaster, men, women and even children began to scramble through the ruins, probing, searching, listening for the piteous cries for help of those still pinned beneath the wreckage. Groups of rescue workers began to work haphazardly.

With the telephone lines dead, the NWMP town picket rode to the police barracks west of town and alerted the station to the disaster. All available men — some 150 in number — were rushed to the scene and with their arrival the work of rescue began to take on a semblance of direction and order. Patrols were immediately set up to curb looting.

Though the CPR telegraph service had been disrupted by the breaking of lines through the freight yards, the wires were re-strung as rapidly as possible and within an hour of the mass tragedy a message crackled out to the world: "Cyclone hit Regina 16:50k. City in Ruins."

The response was immediate and gratifying. By 7:15 that

evening, a special train from Moose Jaw, 40 miles to the west, was unloading doctors, nurses and medical supplies at the Exhibition Grounds, from whence they were rushed by car to the General and the Grey Nuns Hospital. Others were taken to St. Paul's Parish Hall; the Immigration Hall; the Williams Block; the new CNR Freight Sheds; and to the Moore Light Building where emergency treatment centers were being set up to care for the parade of wounded and shocked survivors.

All that night, and for the next two days, wounded Reginians were carried in, or wandered in of their own accord, for belated but necessary medical attention. It was impossible to keep track of the number of injured, and back-weary doctors and nurses numbly bandaged and patched.

Their numbers were augmented when another special train filled with doctors, nurses (and reporters) arrived from Winnipeg the following morning.

With telephone lines dead, with power off and the streets blocked with crumpled buildings, men and women performed miracles of reconstruction as they raced against the fading sunlight. Though the late June sun promised light until the late hours of evening, rescuers were acutely conscious that darkness was fast approaching. All available electricians were pressed into service. Mr. Moore, of Moore's Light Company, placed the full facilities of his warehouse and factory at the disposal of city authorities. And, as men at the power house rushed to restore power, electricians swarmed through the devastated area, cutting wires; restringing them; patching and inventing.

The power came on at 9:00 p.m. in the evening.

With every passing moment the people of the Queen City were beginning to appreciate more fully the viciousness of the twister. They were beginning, too, to notice little things the capricious tornado had done. One man saw a paper photograph driven edgewise into a wall and paused to wonder at it before he went on with the job of digging out more injured. Mr. McConnell, editor of the *Vancouver Sun,* noticed a sliver of wood driven deep into a telephone pole at right angles. In one house he noted that a sectional bookcase had been standing near an open window. The wind had whirled out the central section, leaving the other two intact.

On South Railway Street, a piano case was found — the interior works having been whisked out cleanly. On Smith Street, near the Beelby home, the keyboard and lever-system of another piano lay exposed to the elements. The case had disappeared.

An electric brougham had been standing in front of the King's Hotel and a large splinter of wood had been driven clean through one of the tires — plugging its own puncture. The owner, unable to pull it out, had broken it off short and used the car to transport dead and wounded to the hospitals.

There had been unbelievable escapes — as happens in all natural disasters — and these were as unexplainable as were the deaths and the destruction that happened beside them. At the residence of W. J. Waddell, 1756 Cornwall Street, a Cadillac car had crashed through the front wall into the parlour, where, after striking the opposite wall, it had bounced back again into the street. It just missed Mrs. Waddell. When the walls of the house began falling, Mr. Waddell pulled his wife and son, Albert, into a corner. All three survived and the only serious injury was a broken arm suffered by Albert. Their house was flattened. Just down the street, the Mah Chang Sing Laundry was similarly flattened, with the loss of the lives of Ye Wing and Charlie Sand.

R. G. Williamson, whose house "simply collapsed" expressed the feelings of the survivors succinctly: "How we escaped, I cannot understand."

Although the newspapers which appeared on July 1st, 1912, were unanimous in their belief that "Today will be a day Reginians will never forget," Dominion Days now come and go with seldom a mention of the terrible event. Occasionally, on the June 30th anniversary some enterprising reporter will delve into dusty files in the morgue and come up with a highlight of the event, but by and large, the citizens of the Queen City have forgotten.

Driving down the beautifully shaded Smith and Lorne Streets today, or lolling beside the serene Wascana, or wandering through Victoria Park — which now seems almost hidden by the tall buildings around it, one finds it difficult to believe that one hot, sultry afternoon, when the city was young, these were scenes of horror and destruction. Yet, from time to time, directly south of the prosperous, expanding prairie capitol, little twisters go snarling across the ground — sometimes singly, sometimes in small family groups. Relatively harmless — in comparison to the Grand-daddy of 1912 — these baby tornadoes are recurring reminders that It Could Happen Again!

Red River Rising
Frank Walker

By seven o'clock in the morning of May 4th, the sky over Winnipeg was overcast and there was a threat of rain in the chill air. The temperature was 32 degrees and the cold waters of the Red River, in flood thirteen days, were lapping five feet deep at the east end of Lombard street in the city's heart. The sodden, grey clouds passing overhead were, that afternoon, to turn first into a drizzling rain and then to snow. That Thursday morning, which opened so inauspiciously, was to mark the real beginning of what Colin Herrle, National Director of the American Red Cross, describes as "the worst disaster of its kind in the history of North America".

It was not the start of the flood. That lay far back in a wet autumn and a winter of heavy snow, in a late spring and a sudden thaw. Weeks before the Red River was to reach official flood level in Winnipeg — 18 feet above datum — cities and towns far to the south had been wracked and devastated by the brown water which soon was to cover more than a fifth of greater Winnipeg and send tens of thousands in flight from the city. All that had happened with a monotonous persistence, inch by inch and day by day, and mile by mile; first, the towns of Minnesota, in which state the river rises, then the Dakotas, through which it winds and twists, until finally, fattened by the outpourings of slough and creek, it crossed the international border at Emerson; all this while the water at Winnipeg lay icebound and the city wondered whether there would be a flood and whom to believe.

Even on April 21, when Emerson was preparing for a worse flood than that of 1948, and the river level in the city went over the 18-foot mark, there was no more than a hint of what the future held. The great flood of 1950, though it was conceived in a union of circumstances over many months, was born in a week of rain and snow and wind. The clouds which gathered over the valley on May 4th were the forerunners of disaster. In the days which followed, the isolated battles against the river in defense of a home here and a home there were to become a gigantic struggle for the life of a city, spread over three weeks and riding the headlines of newspapers across the world.

But, on May 4th, though the fight against the flood had already begun on the low land along the river, life in the city was still normal. A dike gave way in the suburb of Elm Park; a few houses on Mayfair avenue were threatened; volunteers were numbered in parties of 60 and 70; the senior boys were diking a private school; the railways were fighting to keep open lines to the south; all this was taking place, but essentially the flow and ebb of the city had hardly felt the ripples of the disaster which lay ahead. Winnipeggers were still reading about the flood, wondering how the people of Morris and St.

Jean and Emerson to the south were getting along, worrying about their basements and going about their business. More than half an inch of rain and 1.2 inches of snow fell that day.

In the glare of lights along Kingston Row, as tired men slipped in the heavy gumbo and cursed the wet snow falling through the leafless trees, there was still hope, that Thursday, that the river, biting at the thin sandbagged dike, could be contained. Houses here had already been surrendered but the retreat had been orderly and, in the language of war, made to previously prepared positions. These hopes were extinguished Friday in the first light of dawn made darker by a thin drizzle and wisps of fog floating over the new breadth of the river. As the day passed, the drizzle turned to rain, low clouds raced overhead and in the hollows of the city the fog persisted. By noon the temperature was only 37 degrees and by evening, as it dropped again close to freezing, the wind rose until it blew a full gale, driving the rain in a glistening curtain across the darker waters of the river.

Downtown the steamheat failed and in three hundred office and factory buildings the chill began to penetrate. Basements were flooded, a radio station went off the air, on street after street pumps belched back onto roads thousands of gallons of evil-smelling water, the reek of which was to hang over the city like the smell of death in the ruined towns of Europe. As the water rose to 25 feet, announcement after announcement broke through the music of five radio stations to call for volunteers. "Supplies of canned milk are urgently needed." "Help is required at St. Boniface sanitarium." "Families are being evacuated from Ferry road, St. Vital." "Those with spare accommodation are asked to contact the Red Cross." "A dike has broken in St. Boniface." "Men are needed at once on Leighton avenue dike." The calls continued throughout the night. Like searchlights prodding through the darkness, the voices of announcers focussed first on this and then on that section of the battle.

Not all the news was defeat. Subway after subway, which had been flooded by the backing up of sewers earlier in the day, was reopened. More troops arrived. On wheelchairs, crutches, on stretchers and by foot, the refugees from the flood moved into the city.

By nightfall the volunteers were gathering in thousands. The town was dressing the part. Rubber boots were the uniform of a new militia. That day 1.34 inches of rain and .2 inches of snow fell in the valley and, where the waters of the river had broadened into lakes, six-foot waves smashed at buildings, carried barns away from their foundations, churned at the insides of abandoned homes and drove the racing waters faster and harder toward the city.

By Saturday morning, though heavy rains still lashed at the border lands seventy miles to the south of Winnipeg, the worst of the storm was over. That evening, for the first time since 7 o'clock Thursday morning, there was a break in the clouds and the stars appeared in the deep blue of a spring sky. But the damage had been done. A vast lake hundreds of miles in extent was forming to the south, and Winnipeg, seen from the air, lay on a belt of land between a rust red sea where the waters of the river had overflowed and the white ice of Lake Winnipeg. That morning, after a night of tension heightened by the urgent voice of the radio and the unceasing roar of the wind, a night of wild confusion on the dikes, of men working knee deep in the sodden clay, of draglines tearing at the soil and bulldozers smashing and ripping their way through trees and bushes, of the evacuation of women and children, of sirens blowing the shrill order˙ to abandon the fight in another suburb, that morning the city woke to feel the flood cutting at its lifelines. The level of the river, at 11 a.m., was 26.4 feet.

Overnight, district after district had been surrendered — Scotia street, Whittier Park, parts of Fort Garry, Point Douglas, the Municipal hospitals, Elm Park. A bridge was closed, a subway. Phones were dead. An army jeep was engulfed by the current. Sleepers awoke to find their homes surrounded by water. A bridge buckled to the south of the city. In the rough water of the lake, even army "ducks" were unable to move. Hotels were jammed with refugees. More troops arrived. Canoeing down a suburban street, one could see furniture floating in what had once been warm and pleasant rooms. By rowboat and motorboat, men were returning to their homes to salvage what they could from the flood. Those whose first floors were still above water were carrying furniture upstairs. At other houses men were smashing at ground-floor windows and pushing aside their floating possessions to enter, while outside chairs and tables and small buildings were bobbing around on the surface in a restless dance which was to continue for weeks.

A city engineer declared the flood "out of hand".

"It is no longer," he said, "a question of defense, but of relief."

That morning Premier Douglas Campbell of Manitoba proclaimed a state of emergency in the Red River valley and placed Brigadier R. E. A. Morton, GOC Prairie Army Command, in charge of the fight against the flood.

"The heavy rains and winds which have prevailed throughout the Red River valley in the past 24 hours have transformed a serious flooding condition into an extremely critical one," said the Premier.

The day of the amateur had ended. From headquarters in the Legislative building the fight against the flood became an organized battle, instead of the guerilla warfare it had been before.

In the next few days — the sun shone that Sunday and lifted the spirits of the city — the corroding influence of the flood slowed and then ceased. Twelve days were to pass before the crest of the flood was reached and another twelve before Army plans to evacuate the entire city were abandoned. Three weeks of anxious waiting and watching lay ahead. More than

100,000 men, women and children in the city and valley were to leave their homes. A huge airlift was to be organized. Millions of sandbags were to pour into the city. The civic auditorium was to be turned into a vast relief centre by the Red Cross. Great ramps of stone and gravel thrown over vital streets to keep open the power stations. Bridges were to be won and lost. The river was to creep higher and higher. There was to be more rain. Men were to work day and night with untiring energy. The report of a women's organization was to show 27,000 hours of work during the three weeks of emergency. Pumps were to be flown in from all parts of the country. Thousands were to be inoculated. Schools were to close and the old and the sick to be moved hundreds of miles to safety. Potholes appeared in the streets and the dust and dirt were to blow in the wind, which came cold and damp to the city over the flood lands to the south. The battle became routine. Dikes were still to go and homes to be flooded. Food and fuel were to be stocked in strategic areas.

But the scenes of Saturday, May 6th, were never to repeat themselves. Suffering and loss were still to come. Old men and old women were to sit, stunned, in the face of disaster, but the fear which mounted to a climax in the storm of May 5th and the grey morning of May 6th was to be throttled in the organization and direction of the days which followed. The lonely isolation of the fight was to be swept away in the flood of help that came from all over the continent. The generosity of thousands was later to show how warm-hearted a nation can be when part of it is facing disaster.

Mercy Flight
Armour MacKay

This is the story of one of the greatest mercy flights ever made in North America. One authority named it, among fifteen years' flights in Canada,"the best, considering the risks of the season and the region". To those two risks one should add the relatively small range of the aircraft used, the absence of radio aids to aerial navigation in the Hudson Bay region in 1939, and the slight chance of rescue if anything went wrong. These risks were recognized when W. E. Catton was nominated for the McKee Trophy, hall of fame of Canadian aviation, for his conduct of the flight.

For some reason the story was not fully reported at the time. Two years after, the record was collected and was read by airmen, Hudson's Bay Company men, and others familiar with the North. Extracts from that account make up this article:

SPECIAL — RACE

DICKINS, WINNIPEG   MONTREAL, 16.04, NOV. 15, 1939

MSGR. TURQUETIL WANTS BADLY INJURED MISSIONARY RUSHED
OUT FROM REPULSE BAY WITH MINIMUM DELAY AS OTHERWISE
MAN WILL BE MAIMED FOR LIFE STOP REALIZES DIFFICULT
CONDITIONS BUT VERY ANXIOUS WE MAKE ATTEMPT STOP PLEASE
ADVISE COST ESTIMATE AND POSSIBILITIES STOP RUSH REPLY

DEBLICQUY

"Punch" Dickins, veteran northern pilot, general superintendent of Canadian Airways, looked up from the radio message and gazed at the big map of Canada that filled a wall of his office.

Repulse Bay!

His eye went up the map — up the whole length of Manitoba, up the west coast of Hudson Bay — Winnipeg and

Lac du Bonnet, God's Lake, Churchill, Chesterfield Inlet, the Arctic Circle — and there, at the last tip of the last northward arm of Hudson Bay — Repulse. Thirteen hundred miles, at the very least.

Repulse Bay! In November! During freeze-up, with the southern lakes too icy for floats, not enough ice yet for skis; with the air full of moisture, to freeze on the wings of an aircraft and rob them of lift, and nothing but forest for a forced landing on wheels. In the dark of the year, with daylight in the Arctic shrinking to three hours in the twenty-four. The west coast of Hudson Bay — the worst flying country in the North — where the company would take no commercial charter from freeze-up till April!

The first blizzards of winter would be sweeping the barrens, wiping out the scanty landmarks, leaving a baffling, blue-white vast in which earth and sky were one, altitude a guess, navigation a game of chance.

He would order no man on such an operation. If the flight were made, it would have to be made by volunteers.

He turned to his desk, wrote swiftly, and called a secretary.

"Tell Montreal we are checking and will answer in the morning. Have the radio query Prince Albert, The Pas, God's Lake and South Trout on landing conditions. Have these men called in . . ."

He returned to the map with scratch pad and ruler. "Lac du Bonnet to God's, 350 miles; God's to Churchill, 300; Churchill to Eskimo Point, 180; Eskimo to Chesterfield, 220; Chesterfield to Repulse, 300." Total, 1,350 miles, one way. Allowing for weather and navigation problems, the return flight would total nearly 3,000 miles. Now, as to fuel . . .

DEBLICQUY, MONTREAL   RACE   10.02 A.M., NOV. 16.
WEATHER PERMITTING CAN PROBABLY MOVE MACHINE IN NEXT
COUPLE DAYS STOP ICE UNSAFE YET AS FAR AS AND AT GOD'S LAKE
AND NO SNOW ON GROUND HERE STOP WEATHER TODAY

GENERALLY ZERO ZERO STOP ADVISE IF MISSION HAS 80 OCTANE
GAS AT LEAST 150 GALLONS ESKIMO POINT 150 GALLONS
CHESTERFIELD 120 GALLONS HAS MISSION A RELIABLE ESKIMO
INTERPRETER AT CHURCHILL OR ELSEWHERE WHO COULD BE
TAKEN ALONG STOP WHAT RADIO STATIONS HAS THE MISSION ON
THIS ROUTE.

DICKINS.

With the message gone to the radio room, Dickins let down.
They would try the flight if necessary. Catton had volunteered
to go, with Hollingsworth as relief pilot and radio man, and
Terpenning as engineer.

Base superintendent at Lac du Bonnet, Bill Catton had
been flying since the first war. "Holly" was post-war, with
experience of two summer operations from Hudson Bay into
the barren lands. Rex Terpenning was the youngest, but with
7,000 or 8,000 miles behind him as engineer on flights on the
Western Arctic coast, winter and summer.

If skill and steadiness could beat the odds against them,
these men would get through. Would the flight be needed?

Two days passed.

DICKINS, WINNIPEG   NOV. 18.
PATIENT AT REPULSE TAKEN TURN FOR WORSE. MSGR. TURQUETIL
REQUESTS TRIP BE ATTEMPTED SOON AS POSSIBLE.

DEBLICQUY.

DEBLICQUY, MONTREAL   NOV. 18.
ARRANGING TRIP. WEATHER PERMITTING PLANE LEAVING
MONDAY.

DICKINS.

R. C. M. POLICE, CHURCHILL   11 A.M., NOV. 19.
REQUESTED MAKE EMERGENCY TRIP TO REPULSE BAY STOP PLEASE
ADVISE MEASURED THICKNESS ICE ON LAKE AND HOW MUCH SNOW
AND SURFACE CONDITIONS STOP WHAT THICKNESS SEA ICE AT

ESKIMO POINT, TAVANE, CHESTERFIELD AND REPULSE BAY AND
LANDING CONDITIONS.

C. H. DICKINS, CANADIAN AIRWAYS

DICKINS, CANADIAN AIRWAYS, WINNIPEG   3 P.M., NOV. 19.
LANDING CONDITIONS AT CHURCHILL IMPOSSIBLE. NO KNOWLEDGE
OF ICE CONDITIONS NORTH.

R.C.M. POLICE.

CANADIAN AIRWAYS, WINNIPEG.   NOV. 21.
OUR AGENT CHURCHILL REPORTS A RAGING BLIZZARD THERE AND
SAYS YOUR PLANE WILL HAVE DIFFICULTY IN FINDING THE
LANDING LAKE.

WIRE CHIEF, CANADIAN NATIONAL TELEGRAPHS.

The three volunteers checked their preparations again.
Aircraft CF-ASN was ready, a single-engined Junkers
monoplane, all metal, low-wing, a rugged type proved by eight
years of service in the North. The fuel in her wing tanks could
take them 300 to 400 miles, depending on the weather.

The equipment was aboard and stowed. SN could carry
1,700 pounds besides the pilot. The load was crowding her
limit.

CANADIAN AIRWAYS, WINNIPEG   NOV. 27.
SN LANDED GOD'S LAKE 11.14.

A hole in the weather had opened that morning, after they
had been held at Lac du Bonnet for a week by fog, rain, sleet
and icing. "The condition of Father Buliard is critical, every
minute counts," the HBC radio was reporting from Repulse
Bay. Could they get there in time?

Three hours after landing at God's Lake, they had jacked
up SN, changed wheels to skis, refuelled, lunched, and were off
again for Ilford, on the Hudson Bay railway, the farthest north
they could make before darkness.

They reached Ilford near sunset, racing a wall of fog that drifted between the tree tops and forced them down on a small lake three miles short of the cabins.

Fog and icing held them on the ground for two days, watching the sky.

The weather opened again on Thursday. They bucked a snowstorm, followed the rails, saw the tree line fade behind them, and sighted the big grain elevator on the snowy tundra at Churchill as the overcast pressed down once more. The sea ice in the harbour was too rough for landing. It was tricky, setting down SN on the little freshwater lake, with the light fading, and she skidded, helpless, across the glare ice. But a snow bank on the far shore brought her up unhurt.

Friday, Dec. 1 — Dawn at Churchill was clear! The thermometer read 25 below. Would the weather hold? It was ten days since the first attempt to take off from Lac du Bonnet, a fortnight since the flight was organized, over three weeks since Father Buliard had frozen his hands. They still were only half way to Repulse, with the most hazardous part of the flight ahead. What of the sick man?

Daylight was bright half an hour before sunrise. Before the 8:55 radio check they were in the air and clear of Churchill. Catton took the aircraft upstairs to 2,500 feet, and levelled off. No use going higher. There was nothing more to see, no matter how high you went. And if the weather closed in, you would need to let down quickly to find a smooth place to land while you could see the surface. Picking a place would take time. The sea ice was too rough, crumpled into pressure ridges. The land was strewn with gravel and boulders, under the snow. The only safe landing place would be some small fresh-water lake. These few lakes, too, were hidden under snow.

Here was the crisis of the flight. Success or failure in the rescue would turn most on the two crossings of this 280 miles of barren flats between Churchill and Tavane. North of

Tavane, the shore was reported to be high enough for landmarks. South of Churchill, you had the railway and familiar country. Here there was just vast whiteness. The navigation and the luck of the weather here would tell the tale.

"The chances are stacked against you." Whose warning was that? "It's easier to get lost there than not. Life's too short for flying around that country in the winter time."

"You might have a forced landing a dozen times and never see a single native camp." That was a Hudson's Bay Company man.

Navigation here would be a gamble. The radio was useful only for weather reports, lacking beam or direction finding equipment. The compass was of little more use, because of areas of magnetic disturbance near Churchill and Tavane. There were no maps of the region for aerial navigation. And the sketchy ground maps might be out fifty to sixty miles in places, "Holly" had found two summers before.

Dead reckoning and landmarks could be the only means of finding the way. And there were no landmarks!

The endless plain of the barrens slipped into the sea in long beaches and tide flats. Snow blanketed the frozen sea and frozen land alike under an endless sheet of white. Shadow or colour change there was none.

"There are no shadows — no contrast — no sensation of distance from the ground. You might be a thousand feet up or you might be only ten," the Hudson's Bay man had said.

Here was the blue-white plain he had described.

One slight line showed in the endless white. The sea ice on the tide flats was pushed into a ridge some miles from shore. Far beyond, at the edge of the floe, the sea was smoking in the cold. Somewhere under this white sheet sea met land with nothing to show the meeting.

They would have to guess a line a few miles inland, and fly there parallel to the line of fog at the floe edge, checking by dead reckoning and the sun, with an eye on the wavering compass and another on the baffling land. If the sun went in, keep your fingers crossed!

SN droned on. The day stayed bright and clear. Soon after ten o'clock, they landed at Eskimo Point for twenty-five minutes, to refuel. Hollingsworth relieved Catton at the controls.

One hundred miles on, the post at Tavane passed beneath the skis. The shore line rose, became rugged, and clear to follow.

Another hour, and a line of vapour rose ahead, where a twelve-foot tide keeps the mouth of Chesterfield Inlet from freezing. At 1:25 p.m., Catton reported "landing at Chesterfield", and reeled in the aerial. A storm was closing in behind. They got through just in time.

Gangrene was spreading on the hands of the sick man at Repulse Bay, they heard at once. It was too late, though, to go farther that day. Night had fallen at Repulse, 300 miles nearer to the Pole. And there was no settlement between, to level a landing strip through the hard-ridged drifts.

The storm that followed SN to Chesterfield had come to stay. Four days of wet snow were followed by another three days of raging gale. But on December 9 the morning broke clear and cold — 25 degrees below.

At 8:40, three quarters of an hour before sunrise, SN was away for Repulse. If the weather held, the round trip might be made in one day. Navigation was easier here. The compass was more unreliable than ever — there were two more magnetic areas to cross, and at Repulse they would be only 300 miles from the Magnetic Pole. But the coast line stood out clearly, the rocky shore rising ever bolder and more rugged. And the risen sun threw long shadows that gave the land perspective.

The mouth of huge Wager Bay passed below, the narrow throat kept free of ice by the great tides.

Half way! And the hour was only 10:15!

Then came head winds. At noon, they were overdue at

Repulse. It was not yet in sight. The sun would set at 1:30 p.m. The engineer was already pumping gas to the wing tanks from the drum in the cabin. And the drum held only eighty minutes' reserve.

Repulse Bay is thirty miles long and quite as wide, cut up into many inlets, with high hills of bare rock between them. Radio signals were not getting through. And they flew along the shores of the bay for half an hour before they spotted four little white-painted buildings, half buried in snow — the HBC post and the mission of Notre Dame des Neiges!

It was 12:30 when SN touched the runway, marked with black coal sacks through the drifts, and taxied to a stop near the buildings — three hours and fifty minutes from Chesterfield.

In her tanks remained only twenty minutes' fuel.

Catton cut the engine, and turned to look at Hollingsworth beside him. Three weeks of care and 1,400 miles lay behind them. The sick man had a chance.

"Damn it, Holly, we're here!"

At the post, they heard of Father Buliard's long ordeal. A young Frenchman, twenty-five years old, with five brothers in the army, Joseph Buliard, O.M.I., left France five months before, had been in the North only since August. On November 6, with the temperature 22 below, he was hunting on the bay three miles from the mission, when the ice broke under him. He was alone. For ten minutes, he struggled in the bitterly cold water before stronger ice bore his weight and he could crawl clear. Both mittens were off, one was lost, and his hands freezing. For an hour he struggled towards help, before he was seen and carried to shelter. Both hands were hard and stiff with frost. There was neither alcohol to wash the frozen hands nor sedative to ease the frightful agony of thawing flesh.

On November 16, three fingers were turning black. Using a kitchen knife, without anaesthetic for the patient, the other priest cut away three pieces of rotting flesh.

Sunday, Dec. 10 — The weather was none too promising. A thick white bank of cloud lay across the southern sky, although it was 30 degrees below. Yet the long grind up the map was ended. They would be flying back now, over country they knew.

They placed Father Buliard in the aircraft and made him comfortable, his hands bundled in cotton wool. The engineer would be at hand, at his flight position in the cabin.

The day lasts only three hours at Repulse Bay in December, with sunrise at 10:30 and sunset at 1:30. At the first flying light, they were away. The cloud bank loomed unbroken. But it lay high, they saw as they neared it, and eventually they passed underneath.

Before sunrise, they were eighty miles south of lonely Repulse. Flying weather here was too precious to lose a minute. Then the red glow ahead turned to gold. The sun rose in the south. Wager Bay faded astern. Heavy overcast pressed down. For an hour, they flew 200 feet above the broken, moving sea ice, wary again of sudden points and hills, until visibility grew wide again, near Winchester Inlet.

Heavy overcast pressed in again as SN neared the frost smoke at the open mouth of Chesterfield Inlet, and the sky grew dull and thick.

But this was a known landing now. At 12:20 p.m., Catton set down SN on the levelled snow near the hospital at Chesterfield three hours from Repulse.

Success! The sick man's life was safe. Soon they would know if his hands, too, could be saved. The crew of SN knew suddenly that they were tired.

The overcast shut down to the rocks. For two days, a blizzard raged.

Wednesday, Dec. 13 — The day begins clear and bright, 15 degrees below, with a north wind to help them south. At dawn they are off. SN makes fast time. Before one o'clock, they are within sixty miles of Churchill. But still they are over the flats.

The wind shifts. The sky thickens, hiding the sun. The land goes blank as a sheet of white paper. A wall of snow comes out of the southwest. . . .

The forced landing is lucky on a small lake behind the beach. The radio aerial is torn away, but nothing worse. Signals still are dead.

An hour goes by. It is 2:40. Sunset is at 3 o'clock here. There is no shelter, and the sick man should not be left to spend the night in the chilling aircraft.

The location is uncertain. If this is Long Point, it does not look like it on the map, but the flying time is right from Eskimo Point, and Churchill and shelter for the sick man are only fifteen minutes away.

Now the falling snow thins out. The overcast is heavy, but visibility is improving. They taxi back along the rough, drifted lake to the landing point, and hope to miss the hummocks. No better runway is in sight.

SN takes off. The air is thick. To get through, they must fly low, and trust the compass, regardless of magnetic disturbance. In the cabin, the engineer checks the time as he watches beside the sick priest.

Twenty minutes have passed. They should be at Churchill . . . Five minutes more . . . SN is over the sea, flying low. Beneath are rough, broken ice floes, crumpled by the thrust of the Churchill river. Ahead there still is water-sky — the dark fog that rises like black smoke from open water.

Ten minutes overdue . . . The light is fading fast. Beneath, waves surge on open water . . . Are they off course, betrayed by the compass? . . . Thirty-five minutes now, since they left the lake. Good thing they refueled at Eskimo Point. Rough ice below. Are they past the open water? The sun set twenty minutes ago. Dusk is gathering. Can they see to set her down, when they reach land? . . . Broken, jagged ice still spreads below.

. . . The grain elevator ahead!

"A very pleasant sight." That was too close to be comfortable!

The weather was dirty all the 300 miles from Churchill to God's Lake — unsettled, with snow flurries. But the ceiling was fairly good. They were back on familiar ground now, with landmarks and tree-sheltered lakes, and could fly safely through poorer weather. But again, the weather went dud.

Wednesday, Dec. 20 — "SN and crew returned from the Repulse Bay trip today, having been held at God's Lake by impossible flying weather since the 15th. Father Buliard was sent immediately to St. Boniface hospital." — *Lac du Bonnet base diary.*

After gathering strength in hospital, the injured priest was sent to Montreal for further treatment. The doctors saved his hands. And in the following August he returned to the mission of Our Lady of the Snows, Repulse Bay. He made the return trip as a passenger on TF, sister ship to SN, piloted again by A. J. Hollingsworth.

Excerpt from a letter by Most Rev. Arsene Turquetil, Vicar Apostolic of Hudson Bay, Jan 3, 1940:

"In connection with this mercy flight to the Arctic Circle, I beg to express anew my high appreciation for the friendliness, sympathy, goodwill and devotion shown to Father Buliard by your men, all along. Rev. Father Ducharme, in charge of the mission at Chesterfield, was very explicit on that. . . . Your aviators, God bless them!"

W. E. Catton, as reported by the Winnipeg Free Press, Dec. 21, 1939:

"The whole trip was uneventful . . . except for . . . weather."

Prairie Fire at Gully Farm
Mary Hiemstra

We did not, of course, always talk of the far future as we jogged over the dry, crisp-smelling grass. Often we talked of the things around us, and I asked innumerable questions. Where had the birds gone? Why did the sky just above the red-and-gold trees look like thin milk? Why were the rabbits turning white?

Dad told me the birds had gone south for the winter, the sky was white because of the haze, and the rabbits were turning white so that they would match the snow when winter came.

Sometimes we talked of Aunt Jane and the little shop, and I longed for a lucky packet: a paper bag that held a whistle, a bit of liquorice, and a few hard candies, and cost only a penny.

"You wouldn't like Littletown now," Dad told me. "All that smoke, and them narrow streets, and no grass to play on."

I didn't disagree with him, at least not out loud, but I would have liked seeing Aunt Jane very much. As for the smoke, there seemed to be quite a bit of it, or something like it, right here. The haze was very thick, and my nose itched the way it did when the stove smoked.

"What shall we do when the prairie fire comes?" I asked, and rubbed my eyes. "Shall we run away?"

"We'll be all right," Dad said, but his eyes narrowed the way they did when he was worried, and he glanced uneasily at the grass. It was very thick and dry, and the gold and orange leaves that still hung on the trees were quite brittle. All the sap had gone out of them, and when I picked a leaf and rubbed it it broke easily. "We have a good wide fire-guard," Dad said as if trying to reassure himself. "Sometimes I think there isn't going to be a prairie fire this year after all. It's near time for snow according to Bill Banks. Another week or two and we'll be safe."

I hoped Dad was right, for we had heard some frightful tales about prairie fires. Sometimes, we had been told, they came at night, and people burned in their beds. Sometimes the smoke smothered them. And they always came fast before you had time to run. "Be sure you have everything ready," the old-timers warned. "Some sacks with hay in the bottom to give them weight, and a barrel of water to wet the sacks in. You won't have much time once the fire starts. There's always a wind, and it comes fast."

We didn't always have a barrel of water, or even a wash-tubful. The slough was almost dry, and we had to get our drinking water from the Metherells. There were sacks in the barn, and hay, but they were dry. As far as I could see the fire-guard was all we had to depend on. It was twelve furrows wide, but prairie fires, it seemed, had a way of jumping.

Mother, who hadn't been sleeping well at nights because she was worried about a fire, always said she would run away when the fire came. She never said where she would run to, but I thought she had a good idea, and intended to run with her.

I was thinking of how my legs would fly through the grass as I outraced the fire when Dad suddenly leaned forward and tightened into a knot. "Look there, Mary," he said, and pointed over the ears of the horses. "Isn't that smoke?"

A puff of yellow cloud was rolling upward behind the distant trees. I stared at it, fascinated. "I don't know," I said.

Even in that small space of time the cloud had grown much bigger, and the lower part of it had burned brown. "It is smoke," Dad said in a queer, tight voice. "The prairie's on fire. Hang on," and he whipped the team and turned them towards home.

"What are you doing back so soon?" Mother asked anxiously when we clattered into the yard.

Dad tried to smile though his face looked pale. "There's a prairie fire coming," he said.

"Where?" Mother looked around. "I can't see any fire."

"You can't see it for the bush," Dad said. "But it isn't far off."

"Well, then, don't stand there looking gormless," Mother snapped. "Let's go and put it out."

"It's too big for that." Dad began taking out the heavy iron pin that held the double-trees to the wagon. "But I'll go and plough a wider guard. You stay in the house with the bairns. You'll be all right."

"The bairns can stay by themselves," Mother said. "I'm going with you."

Dad told her she'd be better off in the house, but Mother paid no attention to him. "Where's them sacks?" she asked, and she ran into the barn and got them.

I helped hitch the horses to the plough, then Mother told me to take Lily and Jack and go into the house.

"You'd better go with them, Sarah," Dad said.

"You'll be better off there. All I have to do is start a back-fire."

"Then let's get on with it." Mother's round face looked frightened but firm.

"Well, all right." Dad shook the reins, and Dad and Mother and the team went around the grove and out of sight.

I took Lily and Jack into the house, and we huddled on the wagon bench for a long time, but the four walls seemed to press in on us, and the unnatural darkness in the middle of the day frightened us. Also, we couldn't see a thing. The fire might be eating up the grove, and we wouldn't know it. I got off the wagon bench, and we all went outside and climbed into the wagon box, and crouched in a corner. We couldn't see any fire, or what was going on at the other side of the grove, but the world was still terrifying.

Rolling clouds of black and brown smoke filled the sky, and stung our noses and eyes. The friendly sun had become an angry red ball that glared at us. Darkness seemed to be closing in, though it was still early afternoon. The wind was hot, and it dropped ashes on us, and skeletons of leaves, and blackened grass. Lily held out her hand and caught a leaf, but it was warm and she dropped it.

I brushed the ashes out of Jack's fair hair, but more kept falling. The whole sky seemed full of ash, wind, and smoke, and we were alone in the turmoil. Mother and Dad had forgotten us.

After a while Lily began to cry, and even Jack, who was only about a year old, looked pale and frightened. Had the fire burned Dad and Mother? I recalled some of the stories I had heard. Prairie fires often jumped fire-guards and burned houses and people. Perhaps this fire had burned Mother and Dad and was now coming to burn us. The smoke was much thicker than it had been, and the wind hotter. "Let's go to the Metherells," I said, remembering that once Mother had told me to go there if she didn't come back from the slough.

Lily said, "All wite" and dried her eyes with her fists, and we scrambled out of the wagon box. It was supported on two or three logs, and was quite a drop for Jack, but he made it without any trouble.

I took one of Jack's little hands — he could walk by then — and Lily took the other, and we started off. We followed the little path that went around the grove, rubbing the smoke out of our eyes, and fully expecting to be safe and out in the friendly sunshine again once we were away from the trees that seemed to be holding the smoke and wind. But when we rounded the corner of the grove a terrible sight met us. Flames were everywhere. They stretched from grove to grove, jagged rows of fire much taller than I was, and all an angry orange-red. While we watched open-mouthed, the flames leaped high into some trees and licked at the bright leaves, turning them into black ash, then they dropped back to the cringing earth, leaving the trees bare and smoking, and began gobbling up the underbrush and the late asters.

The wind was almost as vicious as the fire. It tossed burning branches high in the air, fanned the flames into a wild dance, and hurled the smoke at us. It stung our eyes, and scraped our throats and made us cough, but worst of all it felt like a hot hand close on my face.

Lily and I stood still in the little trail and looked at each other.

We were too frightened to speak. The whole world seemed to be on fire. We didn't know what to do.

Suddenly, as if she knew we needed her, Mother came out of the smoke, but she looked so unlike the pretty Mother we were used to we were almost afraid of her. Her face was black, and her eyes were red. Her hair was singed, and so were her eyelashes and brows. "Where are you going?" she called.

"To the Metherells' away from the fire," I shouted.

"There's fire at the Metherells', too. You'll be burned to death if you try to go there. Go back home, and be quick." And without waiting to see whether we obeyed or not she went back into the smoke.

We were more than glad to do as we were told. Hurrying as fast as we could we returned to the wagon box, climbed in, and crouched there too frightened to even move, and at last the fire came around the corner of the grove.

Driven by the wind a spear of flames began to eat up the grass in the little glade between our grove and the one nearest to it. The flames bent before the wind and took a bite of grass, then they straightened up for a moment, and weaved and swayed as they swallowed their mouthful. It was a terrible but fascinating sight. Lily's brown eyes, just above the rim of the wagon box, bulged, and her little face was white under its film of ash.

I suppose my face was white, too, and I know I shivered though I wasn't cold, but I made no effort to go into the house or even speak. I simply stood there practically paralysed with fear and fascination.

Jack huddled between Lily and me and didn't whimper

even when hot ash fell on his face. Most of the ash and skeletons of leaves was warm by then, and once or twice a smoking twig fell in the wagon box, but fortunately they did no damage. What we would have done if Dad and Mother hadn't come I don't know: probably stood there watching the fire until we were burned to death.

Dad and Mother, however, came around the grove while the fire was still some distance away. They were half hidden by smoke, and they looked like dolls in some terrible dream. Mother was driving the team and doing very well at it. She was running and her long, wide skirts streamed out behind her, and so did the little shawl tied around her neck. When they came to the edge of the fire-guard Dad righted the plough with a jerk, and the excited horses paused for a second, then, their backs bent and their legs stiff, they plunged forward.

There was only time to plough two furrows between Mr. Gardiner's fire-guard and ours before the fire came dangerously close, but Dad and Mother didn't stop fighting even then. Dad tipped the plough on its side, snatched a handful of grass, lit it, and started back-firing. Mother drove the team close to the house, then, without even taking time to tie the horses, or glance at us, she ran to help Dad with the back-fire.

A back-fire is set along the edge of a fire-guard, a road, or some other obstacle. Having to burn against the wind it does not burn as fast as the wind-driven fire, and is much easier to control. The flames next to the guard are put out if they threaten to cross, the other side burns towards the oncoming fire, and they finally meet and burn out.

Dad and Mother had to work quickly, but they had to be careful, too. The wind was strong, and the two furrows only a narrow guard. Dad dragged a handful of burning grass for three or four yards, then, with their weighted sacks ready, he and Mother watched it. If the flames began to blow across the guard they beat at them until they went out. As soon as they had burned one little strip they started on another. It was exciting work. Dad tried to start each little section of fire when there was a lull in the wind, but a sudden gust sometimes caught the little back-fire and whipped it into a blaze. At times Mother and Dad were lost in smoke, and often the flames seemed to lean over and touch them. Once the fire leaped the guard, and Dad and Mother beat frantically until they got it out. They couldn't, of course, put the main fire out. All they could do was save our house, the grove beside it, and a little grass for the horses to eat.

Dad and Mother watched the fire until it had passed Mr. Gardiner's fire-guard, then, when they were sure his little house was safe, they came slowly home, dragging their blackened sacks. Lily, Jack and I were still clinging to the edge of the wagon box too stiff to move, even though we knew the danger was over. Afterwards Mother said she would have laughed when she saw us if she hadn't been so tired, and so glad we were safe. She said we looked queer: three little noses, three pairs of eyes, and six little hands was all she could see above the rim of the wagon box.

Mother and Dad looked queer, too. Their faces were black, they had neither eyelashes nor eyebrows, and they were covered with ash from head to foot. The only clean thing about them was their eyeballs, and they looked like pale, red-rimmed marbles. Mother got quite a shock when she tried to hug Jack. He didn't recognize her and clung to me and cried.

But terrible as Dad and Mother looked, the prairie looked far worse. The grove beside Mr. Gardiner's house and the one beside ours were still there, plus a little grass between, but all the rest of the prairie as far as we could see was charred and black. The trees that had been so lovely in their red and gold leaves were stark and bare. The tall blue asters and the golden-rod were only burned sticks, and the grass that had been a thick grey carpet and soft to walk on was now black and smoking ash. It seemed incredible that the prairie, lovely in its fall colours only this morning, was now a dark and dismal desolation. I looked at the poplars naked against the sky, at the shivering willows, and the consumed rosebushes, and tears washed the ashes off my cheeks. "Everything will grow again in the spring," Mother said when I told her why I was crying, but I wasn't comforted. Spring seemed a long time away.

Dad and Mother had barely wiped the ash from their faces when the Metherells and Bill came to see how we had fared. They brought us some water because they knew we hadn't much, and Dad lit the fire, and Mother filled the kettle. While we waited for the kettle to boil we sat outside on the woodpile looking at the smoking desolation and the far-away fire that still winked in the gathering twilight.

I didn't see Mr. Gardiner come, but after a while he was there. Everybody seemed to talk at once in happy, excited voices. The Metherells had saved their house and barn. It had been touch-and-go once or twice, but they had won. Dad and Mother had won, too, and they looked at one another with a new light in their smoke-reddened eyes, and a new pride on their smeared faces. The old-timers, who had predicted that the greenhorns would be burned out when the first prairie fire came, had been proved wrong. "There's good stuff in the Barr Colony no matter what they say," Mrs. Metherell said proudly.

"Especially in the women," Dad said, his thin face one big smile. "You ought to have seen Sarah lambasting that fire. The way she swung that sack! I was glad it wasn't me she was hitting. And telling me she was scared of fire! She fair laid into it."

"It wasn't because I wanted to," Mother said, but she smiled happily. "I beat because I had to, and I hope I never have to do it again."

"Nell did a good job." Mr. Metherell smiled at his wife. "As a matter of fact she told Bill and me what to do."

"I did not." Mrs. Metherell's green eyes sparkled. "I only told you to get the blazes out of the house when I saw the fire coming."

"Well, we know now that we don't have to bother about the women," Dad said, his ocean-flecked eyes sparkling. "If they say they're scared we'll know they're having us on. The way Sarah tackled that fire, I bet she could best anything. And she thought she wasn't pioneer stuff."

"And I'm not," Mother said firmly. "And I'd rather be where there are no prairie fires to fight."

"Same here." Mrs. Metherell tilted her chin a little, and she and Mother went into the house to make tea.

After they had washed the ashes out of their throats with several cups of tea, and discussed the fire at length, our visitors went home, but they did not take the happy exultation with them. It filled our house, and lived with us for a long time, and while it was there Mother never mentioned going back to England.

The Fire

Eric Nicol

If there is one day of the year that deserves to be named "Vancouver Day" — as indeed it was, officially, in 1925 — it is June 13. It was on a June 13 that Vancouver, the site, was first seen by Captain George Vancouver. On a June 13 the survey ship *Plumper* discovered the coal seam that attracted attention to the inlet. And on June 13, 1886, Vancouver was lost, in the Fire.

Other cities — Rome, London, Chicago, San Francisco — had their histories glamorized by a great fire, but none has been as precocious in the accomplishment as Vancouver, which only two months after its incorporation lay a smoking waste. If it is the first intimation of a city's greatness that it burns itself down, Vancouver lost no time in qualifying for fame.

The student of Vancouver's first civic election may be

excused for assuming that the Fire was the direct result of the city's becoming emotionally overheated, spontaneous combustion sparked by politics whose alcoholic content made it highly flammable. The causes of the Fire were otherwise, and more awesome than the isolated accident of Mrs. O'Leary's cow kicking over the lantern. No Nero fiddled while Vancouver burned. The holocaust drew inspiration not from a sly emperor but a shifty wind. And its strength had been years in the making, a colossal bonfire, built around a stake of spar tree, by the men who were to be martyrs to their own transcendent stupidity.

By 1886 the immediate environs of Vancouver had been logged. Some of the finest timber on the entire coast had stood at the crest of what is now the heart of downtown Vancouver, the Pacific Centre-Bay store area. One Douglas fir that stood on Georgia Street between Seymour and Granville was reported to be thirteen feet in diameter at the stump. The fallen giant was measured as four feet thick at a distance of two hundred feet from the butt, sections of which were shipped home to a British garden show as a colonial phenomenon.

The method of logging the area that is today's business section and West End was, to put it as charitably as possible, rude. The loggers chopped only one side of the trunks of the smaller trees, Gallagher recounts, "and then let a big tree fall down upon them; the whole thing would go down with a crash, like a lot of ninepins." This domino method of forest husbandry was soon improved upon: "As the felling progressed southwards towards Davie Street — they started from Burrard Inlet and worked south — a whole section of ten or more, perhaps twenty, acres would go down with one great sweeping crash. The axemen cut down firs and cedars only; the smaller trees were knocked down, crushed, smashed."

Such was the scene of silvi-slaughter come upon by the crews hired by the CPR to clear the area for the new terminus and attendant land development. "People of today may gather some conception of the general appearance of all that tract mentioned," says Gallagher, "if they will imagine brush, limbs and timber to a depth of ten feet or more lying strewn over the ground in an almost solid mass in every direction. . . ."

The stage was set for the melodrama of revenge. On June 13, 1886, the curtain — among other things — went up. In the best tradition of dramatic irony, those who actually initiated the disaster were relatively innocent, except to those convinced that the CPR could do no right. That the railway gaveth, and the railway tooketh away, was true of this event insofar as the Fire started where the CPR men were clearing the site of the roundhouse. The land-clearing operations, the burning of stumps and debris, had been under way for some time west of the settlement. The citizenry had become accustomed to the pall of smoke that dimmed the June sun into a deceptively pale disk. The feckless population was increasing daily with the influx of drifters and get-rich-quick artists attracted by the prospects of a boom town, transients in whose nostrils the smell of loot was too strong for them to notice the atmosphere redolent of Gomorrah chastised.

The spring had been dry. The humidity level was at that low point where men who work in the woods, who know the woods, do not burn, do not so much as touch off an oath, but keep their snoose moist and spit where it is driest. The CPR crew burned slash, at a distance from the main tangle of forest wreckage, taking the calculated risk that there would be no sudden change in direction or force of the breeze. The blazes they played were tigers, unpredictable, making sudden rushes, waiting for the split second of situation in which the trained servant becomes the master fury, striking swift, deadly and implacable.

It was a Sunday. Shopkeepers, some of them, had taken temporary leave of their livelihood, and of the stock and records for which the small businessman would risk his life in the effort of rescue. This dislocation assured the running in opposite directions essential to fullblown panic. Many of the absentees were fortunately as far removed as New Westminster, attending a funeral, a rare instance of the dead saving the quick and a harsh moral lesson to those who failed to pay their respects. For generations afterward a Vancouver Sunday reflected this debt to the deceased.

About 2 p.m. of that Sunday afternoon in June the forces of violated nature swung into attack. The wind veered and gained velocity. The crews tending the fires made a frantic effort to smother the blazes whose sparks were showering into the tinder-dry wasteland of wood, then fled for their lives.

Accounts of what happened in the next frenzied forty-five minutes, during which the town was reduced to a few acres of red-hot embers several feet deep, are as various as the individuals that survived it. But none comes closer to the epic style of Virgil describing the immolation of Troy than that of the *Daily News* of June 17. Burned out, the newspaper required only four days to find its voice, on borrowed New Westminster presses, and chronicle as stirring a story of disaster as ever moved the bowels of journalism. Even the typography catches the faltering flight of the fire's victims, each subhead a dramatic shout among the smoke-streaked columns of type. If the comparison to Pompeii strikes the reader as extravagant, it must be remembered that in 1886 the Roman antecedent was still very incompletely excavated.

THE FIRE

Probably never since the days of Pompeii and Herculaneum was a town

WIPED OUT OF EXISTENCE

so completely and suddenly as was Vancouver on Sunday. . . . It was about two o'clock in the afternoon that the breeze which had been blowing from the west

BECAME A GALE,

and flames surrounded a cabin near a large dwelling to

the west of the part of the city solidly built up. A few score men had been on guard with water and buckets, between this dwelling and the cabin, but when the wind became a gale they were forced to

FLEE FOR THEIR LIVES,

and in a few minutes the dwelling was a mass of flames and the whole city was filled with flying cinders and dense clouds of smoke. . . .

The ubiquitous Gallagher, who was a railway contractor by trade, returned to his office, leaving three of his men to fight the fire, which according to his recollection broke out earlier, "before 10 a.m.

> I secured our books and money; pay day was nearing, but there was not much time; I had been in our little office but a few moments when I saw, through the window, a rabble of people running by. They were coming down Hastings Road, from the direction of the Deighton House, Gassy Jack's place. I went out on the road, walked up towards Gassy Jack's, but by the time I got there the Sunnyside Hotel across the street was a mass of flames, and before I could get back to the office I had just left, that was on fire too; I had not even time to save clothing.

Gallagher saved himself by wading into the harbor and sucking air close to the surface of the water.

> The city did not burn; it was consumed by flame; the buildings simply melted before the fiery blast. As an illustration of the heat, there was a man driving horse and wagon, caught on Carrall Street, between Water Street and Cordova Street; the man and horse perished in the centre of the street. The fire went down the sidewalk on old Hastings Road, past our office, so rapidly that people flying before it had to leave the burning sidewalk and take to the road; and the fire

travelled down that wooden sidewalk faster than a man could run.

"The only time I remember being scared was when the roof blew off the soda water factory," recalled Mrs. W. E. Draney later. Then a little girl living with her family on Pender near the rail crossing, she was nearly incinerated when her father made the near-fatal misjudgement of going to the stable to fetch a wagon for their belongings. "The first thing we knew we were surrounded by fire. Father took us to the back of the lot and we crouched down in a hollow. He kept wetting blankets in a pond or stream and putting them over us. He had to keep it up for three quarters of an hour." Mrs. Draney, at the time two years old, had her hair badly burned when a flying ember pierced the blanket.

Those who had a choice other than staying put fled to the nearest large body of water: either inlet, if they happened to be on the north side of town, or False Creek, if they were caught to the south. One of those who retreated north was volunteer firefighter George Cary, who very quickly gave up the unequal struggle: "Chunks of flaming wood as big as my legs were flying clear over us and dropping in the town. I gathered up a mother and two children from a shack behind the hotel and started east, but all Water Street was ablaze. So we turned back and scurried down to an old float at the foot of Cambie and waded into the inlet. The tide took a raft near me and I grabbed it. The mother said something about throwing the children into the sea because she would rather see them drown than burn. Then a boat came in and pulled the raft out."

Black Joe Fortes was also in the thick of the fight to save the distraught. Yet another of the firefighters later described the scene with a metaphorical *feu de joie:* "The fire apparatus had not arrived. The country west of Cambie Street was a mass of trees, and on that day becoming a screaming tub of fire, from which flame tentacles reached out and licked up the village like bits of paper."

Such a conflagration was of course the cynosure of all eyes on the North Shore, where many of the Indians rushed to their canoes with the intent of aiding in the rescue of their neighbours across the inlet. According to the curious tale of a witness, they were deterred by the mission priest, who stood on the beach, face ruddied by the glow across the water, and said: "No, my children. The white man will lose many things in this fire. If you go you may be blamed by some bad man for stealing. Who knows?"

More verifiable is the fact that the hundreds of people who fled before the Fire straight into the waters of the inlet had no choice other than swim or burn. Captain Soule's ship, the old *Robert Kerr,* lay at anchor off the beach. No wharf led to the ship, but the small boat-landing held a number of oared craft such as canoes that were quickly commandeered for the short haul to the ship. A watchman aboard the sailing ship tried to object to the boarders with what the *News* described as "insect authority", but was in short order persuaded to be hospitable to the 150 to 200 persons who scrambled over the rail. Those who could not find a boat, or were poor swimmers, rolled logs down from the beach into the water, and frantically paddled out of range of the searing heat.

People whom the Fire caught on the False Creek side of the peninsula had some of the more harrowing escapes. As the *News* reported:

 . . . John Boultbee and C. A. Johnson saved their lives by lying down and
BURROWING THEIR FACES
in the earth. Both are still suffering from their injuries.

 . . . Many men were completely crazed, and did not recover their senses for hours. . . .

Indeed, some of the behavior in the moment of crisis was

singularly odd. For example, a storekeeper who was running to the rescue of his stock passed a shop window in which a baby was sitting, apparently deserted. The storekeeper then saw the mother sitting nearby, paralyzed with fear. Breaking open the door he snatched up the baby to carry it outside. The mother at once struggled with him, screaming that the child could not go outside without its shoes on. He broke away from the hysterical woman and saved the baby. Luckily, a week later he was able to return the child to its mother, given up for dead but in fact taken across the inlet to Moodyville.

The same storekeeper (A. M. Herring, who had come from New Westminster by horse and buggy to visit his branch drugstore, and who had left his family at the Bridge Hotel at the end of False Creek bridge) on the same street passed two men carrying a wire bedspring and mattress. One was moaning, "Oh, my poor wife, my poor wife!" When Herring asked the man what had happened, the man replied that he had had to leave the good woman behind, to certain death. Asked why he did not return to save her, the man cried: "I can't let go of this mattress, can I?"

In the moment of truth a man's values become incandescent. Another witness saw a man race back into the flames to save a dead goose. Yet another helped to drag a man from the roof of his house, which he was dousing with water from two small tins. A pioneer who had a piano box in his back yard hurriedly filled it with books, silverware and clothing, nailed up the piano box with a hatchet and lit out down the trail to New Westminster carrying the hatchet, which survived.

With equal presence of mind a citizen threw a bundle of books down a well. They drowned.

Most poignant sight of all, if it is to believed, was that of the Vancouver homeowner who at the height of the inferno went out of his mind and died trying to save his stock of firewood.

As the *News* reported with accuracy, the total number of victims and their identity will probably

NEVER BE KNOWN

With the exception of Mrs. Nash and Mr. Craswell, the bodies recovered were all burned to crisp and barely recognizable as human remains. Mr. Craswell's body was found in a well wherein he took refuge and died of suffocation. A young man named Johnson, and his mother, were found in the same well. Johnson was dead and Mrs. Johnson has since died. The body of Mr. Fawcett, the soda water manufacturer, was identified by his wife by means of his watchchain.

Druggist Herring, having rescued as many reluctant survivors as he could persuade to abandon the prospect of certain death, returned to the Bridge Hotel, whose location at the end of the False Creek bridge spared it from destruction. He assisted in comforting the burned and homeless as they straggled in during the long afternoon. As there was no first-aid equipment available, those who manned the makeshift receiving station tore up skirts and shirts for bandages. "I did manage to find some flour, linseed oil and some big skunk cabbage leaves," Herring reported, and the poultice was effective enough to support the claim that what the laurel was to Rome, such to Vancouver is the skunk cabbage.

Soon help began to arrive from New Westminster. From Port Moody, the antagonist town, four sailors, as soon as news of the fire reached them, loaded medical supplies into a rowboat and rowed, part of the way against the tide, the full distance to the stricken Vancouver waterfront. They were rewarded with fried egg sandwiches packed by a New Westminster woman.

Mayor MacLean sent messengers to groups of survivors asking these to assemble at the south end of Westminster Avenue, just over the bridge. Says Gallagher:

Mayor MacLean's call to assemble was followed by what was probably the sorriest looking procession Vancouver ever had, and I hope ever will see, and long to be remembered by those who witnessed it. Hungry and temporarily despondent women, children and men, who had lost all they possessed, some even their clothes, straggled in in twos, threes or larger groups, along that rough old trail, through the woods in the blackness of that dark dreary night, and gathered together to await the arrival of food.

The coming of darkness and its chill added to misery and confusion. "A man with a blanket that night was wealthy," says Darrel Gomery *(A History of Early Vancouver)*. Many survivors simply wandered all night, too dazed to respond to weariness. More than a hundred slept on the ground in a clearing at the south end of the Westminster Avenue bridge. In the morning, their demands on the water pump of the Bridge Hotel caused the owner to chain it for fear the well would go dry — a precaution that nearly got him tarred and feathered.

The hotel became an improvised morgue as bodies began to be removed from the smoldering ruin of Vancouver. Gallagher:

We gathered together some bits of board and built a table about three feet high, five feet wide, and thirty feet long, and as each body, or part of body, was brought in, it was reverently laid upon that table. Some bodies had not an arm, nor foot, nor head left; some of the poor remains would not hold together; some weighed a few pounds, perhaps twenty or thereabouts; all had so suffered by fire that they were not recognizable. The Bridge Hotel gave us their blankets, and on these were wrapped such remains as were found, with a little note attached to each parcel saying where the contents were picked up. Altogether there were twenty-one parcels, and I know of others, those which were not discovered until the work of clearing away the debris of the burned buildings began. . . .

The grisly business of collecting the remains of the fire's victims had its touch of macabre humor. On that Sunday Dr. H. E. Langis of the CPR construction medical service was out of town, and the human skeleton that was one of the appointments of his office had been temporarily placed in McCartney's store. "After the fire they picked it up in the ashes," Langis later told archivist Major Matthews, "and took it to the morgue. And do you know what I am told they said when they picked it up? 'Poor fellow, he must have been sick before he died — his back is all wired together.' "

Alderman Gardiner Johnson witnessed one of the more agreeable aspects of the relief work: the distribution of underwear to women. "I remember when a carload of whitewear of this description arrived. The women used to come to the relief tent for a pair of corsets or something else white, and securing things, they would run off into the bush to try them on. If they fitted they came back smiling, but if they did not fit, another trial had to be made in the bushy boudoir."

The dawn light of the morning after revealed the full devastation of the fire. Every structure, every living thing above ground and for a foot below it, had been effaced, except for the Hastings Mill buildings, the Regina Hotel on Abbott and Water streets — a freak survival thanks to a change of wind direction — and the Bridge Hotel with its eight or ten smaller buildings on False Creek. Another odd exception to the rule of rubble: a survivor climbed a mound of smoldering sawdust to scan the horizon for a brother who was missing. His feet slipping on the sawdust, he fell and was astonished when his hands encountered ice beneath the charred chips.

The Sunnyside Hotel's supply of ice had been preserved when the icehouse collapsed and dropped its insulation of sawdust atop the ice blocks. Thus some of the first water Vancouver drank after the fire was ice water.

West of the fire zone, the Spratt's fish warehouse and the CPR offices were untouched — further irony, in view of what started the fire. Of the buildings destroyed — numbered upwards of six hundred to perhaps a thousand — few were insured, and those only for a fraction of their value. The fire tempered the crude steel of frontier spirit into pioneers more provident.

By three a.m. on Monday, however, the first tent had been pitched on the still-warm cinders of Vancouver. From dawn onward wagons loaded with lumber rumbled down the baked streets. R. H. Alexander, the defeated candidate for mayor, rose to the occasion splendidly, inviting all who needed lumber for rebuilding to help themselves to sawn lumber stacked in the mill yards. Within three days a dozen firms, including a clothing store, a three-story hotel, a public hall and a hardware shop, were doing business in jaunty if jerry-built quarters; and four hundred houses would be erected during the next three months.

Typical of the poise with which Vancouver's people recovered from the disaster is a morning-after photo of survivors in which, according to the caption, "Walter E. Gravely, [later well known in financial circles], lies reading on the ground." Reading what? The casual reclining does not suggest Scripture. The mind has difficulty conceiving the kind of aplomb that enjoys a little light reading, alfresco, a few hours after Herculaneum.

Another sign of how coolly the phoenix would arise flapping from its own ashes was the resurrection of Vancouver's City Hall. In a letter, L. A. Hamilton describes the deed: "In all history, no City Hall has been built more rapidly than the one I erected in five minutes the morning after The Fire. We got a tent. I was senior Alderman. I got a can of paint, a brush and a piece of board, and labelled it 'City Hall'. We held Council meetings in it; a magistrate's court sat there; at the foot of Carrall Street at Water Street."

The panoply of spreading canvas, and its occupying

dignitaries, were captured in one of the aftermath photos. Unfortunately no pictorial record exists of the prisoners, released from jail during the fire, who were chained to stakes beside the tent that was City Hall. The felons had taken advantage of their sudden parole by breaking open whiskey kegs and enjoying the civic house-warming too well. A witness described the flimsy bastille: "Its white canvas sides stood out against the blackened embers to whisper to the people that, though the city was in chaos, yet were the steel muscles of the law tensed in readiness to enforce the Queen's commands."

Except for the drunks, the sinewy servants of law and order were not called upon to cope with much in the way of mischief. Everybody was too busy rebuilding to have time for disturbing Her Majesty's peace. That most of the population had escaped the fate of their homes and chattels lent to the work a gratitude to Providence which had formerly been negligible in Vancouver's devotions. One minister appraised the Fire as a blessing in that it occurred "on the day that the Church was celebrating the coming down of the Holy Spirit under the outward symbol of tongues of fire."

The first church service on the Sunday following the Fire was an impromptu but, according to Gallagher, memorable ceremony:

> Rev. Mr. Thompson, the Presbyterian clergyman, came along, and suggested to the workmen who were grading Cordova Street and covering it with planks — three by twelve planks — that perhaps they ought to cease work for a moment, and give thanks to the Almighty for the escape the previous Sunday. Everyone in sight laid down their tools; the teamsters left their horses standing. Then they picked up the empty spike kegs, and some planks, and carried them into an empty store in process of erection for Geo. L. Allen, the boot and shoe merchant, and made rows of seats out of the kegs and planks. About one hundred and fifty went in to the service.

Just at that moment His Worship Mayor Maclean came along, and he joined in the simple yet deeply impressive service. The men were, of course, in their working clothes; the service was not long, and was soon over. At its conclusion those big, rough, hardy bushmen paid as gentle a compliment as ever I have witnessed. The service over, none moved; they all stood motionless while His Worship moved down the rude aisle. His Worship halted at the entrance, and stood to one side; Rev. Thompson on the other, and both shook hands with each member of the impromptu congregation as they slowly departed from the half-finished building. Then the men went back to work to make Cordova Street passable.

As sustenance for the body, the Hastings Mill Store experienced a dramatic run on stock and was soon down to its large reserves of soda crackers. Some veterans of the Fire suffered no permanent injury except a lifelong aversion to soda crackers.

Nearby, another lucky survivor was the home of the Jones family, whose telephone kept Vancouver in touch with New Westminster, the house becoming the city's temporary telephone office.

More permanent structures were soon under way. The same June 17 edition of the *Daily News* that reported the Fire also published a list of new buildings already begun four days after it — including a photographic gallery. Along with the abundance of photos of the period, this haste in providing a photographic gallery points up the narcissism that is part of Vancouver's personality. Few places have been more in love with their own image, or more willing to believe, like Dorian Gray, that excesses and self-indulgence would be reflected only in the portrait.

One week after the Fire the city council passed a building bylaw requiring more solid construction than heretofore. Soon buildings of brick and stone were rising as replacements of the wooden Topsies that just grew. For the next decade Vancouver was to build with an emphasis on durability unknown before or since. Some of the sturdiest structures of brick and stone in North America remain as evidence of the architectural concepts inspired by flames licking at the heels. They may lack the grace of the Acropolis, but they are fully competitive in endurance.

George Brown's *Herald* was among the irrepressible enterprises that soon found new premises, as Cordova, Water and Carrall streets filled with fourteen office blocks, twenty-three hotels, fifty-one stores, nine saloons, one church, two stables, one wharf, one mill, and one skating rink, all completed by the end of 1886. Also by the end of that momentous year the population of Vancouver had soared to five thousand persons, inhabiting completed construction valued at $521,000, and waiting impatiently for uncompleted buildings worth another $524,000. Tinderbox though the great fire had proven the city's physical presence to be, Vancouver's confidence in itself was firmly packed in asbestos.

Jimmy Was No Hero!
Marion Brooker

Jimmy was no hero! At least he didn't feel like a hero. Certainly, as he fished Palaya Ashevak from the icy waters off Cape Dorset with a sealing hook, becoming a hero hadn't crossed his mind. Even now, as Governor General Vanier pinned the bronze cross on his Boy Scout shirt, Jimmy was thinking "Here am I, a twelve year old Eskimo boy 1800 miles from home. I'm receiving one of the highest honors a Scout can and all I hope is that *I don't do something stupid during this ceremony!*"

Jimmy heard himself being introduced as Jimmy Teegodlegak from Cape Dorset. It sounded strange. To Jimmy

Cape Dorset would always be *King-Aik* which in his language means "high land".

Winter swoops in early in *King-Aik* like a magpie diving on a dog's bowl. It grabs hold and hangs on for many months. There was something friendly and quiet about *King-Aik* during the winter months. The adults talked about how it used to be during those long dark days when ships could no longer come into the harbor and visitors had returned to their jobs in the south. The days passed slowly. Certainly, his people had always loved carving from soapstone but now that the Co-operative had been formed there was purpose to their carving. The winter months passed happily preparing carvings, parkas and sealskin boots to be sold throughout the world. The men in *King-Aik* would go out on hunting trips in search of white fox, polar bear, wild fowl and caribou. Nowadays, they often returned shaking their heads. The white fox was disappearing. They were sad at the loss of a livelihood. They were sad at the loss of such a beautiful animal — lithe as it sped across the tundra.

But as the grasp of winter loosens its hold on the settlement, his people appear from everywhere and from nowhere — like people when they hear a marching band. The music which calls his people out of their winter hibernation is the noise of cracking ice which carries long distances on the still crisp air. One day they stop to breathe in the warming air and in the distance they hear the first sound of spring. To the Eskimo the sound of the ice beginning to loosen in the Bay is like the sight of the first robin to a child farther south. But as you know it is a long time from the first sight of a robin until you pick a sweet-pea from the garden, so the children in *King-Aik* realize that from the first cracking of the ice until the Bay is completely free from icepans will take some time.

It was very late the night of July 5. Adults and children alike were gathered on the beach. There were two reasons why children were still up. Holidays had come and Eskimo parents are not slaves to a clock. Also, in *King-Aik* at this time of the year the sun sinks very slowly and the sky rarely becomes totally dark. It is the land of the midnight sun. Adults visited. Children skipped stones across the water and if the adults weren't watching some of the more daring jumped from ice pan to ice pan near the shore. This was forbidden at this time of the year as the ice pans had become dangerously small and thin. The Bay was almost clear of them. From Salisbury Island in the Inlet the funny, sandpapery noises of the walruses floated across. One old man held a duck he had been carving from soapstone. It was wrapped now in a soft skin.

"May I see it?" Jimmy asked. It was heavy. Jimmy ran his hand over the carving. It was perfectly smooth. Jimmy knew the hours it had taken the old man to shape the head so gracefully; to give the gentle flip to the tail. What he loved was its simplicity. The duck was without markings except for the eyes. The eyes were the tip of a bird's wing which had been set into the stone.

"Someday I may be an artist" Jimmy thought "and stay right here in *King-Aik.*"

"Help! He . . . lp!" shattered the evening quiet. The people on shore jumped up. They listened. All was still again. It was that dusky time of night when it's almost harder to see than when the sky is pitch black. They searched the dusk for a form. Was it merely some boy playing a joke on them?

"Help!"

That was no joking call!

Then quiet.

Splashing.

"Someone's slipped off an ice pan. Someone's drowning," shouted Pudloo, racing towards the water.

Jimmy was right behind.

"He . . .lp!"

They followed the sound, turning their heads and listening, to locate it exactly.

"It's Palaya," shouted Jimmy. "He was playing on ice pans near the shore."

"He's gone out too far and fallen off," Pudloo yelled over his shoulder as he searched the water for an ice pan big enough to hold an adult. "And in that icy water . . ." His voice trailed off. Suddenly he spotted a large ice pan. Quicker than the white fox he hunted, Pudloo was onto the only pan large enough to hold him. He held! He shifted his weight from one foot to the other to set the pan in motion. It wouldn't budge. He tried paddling with his hands. The pan didn't move.

It took Jimmy only an instant to realize that Pudloo was going nowhere. In the same instant he realized that if Palaya was to be saved it would have to be by a child, not an adult. *And fast!* Jimmy hesitated for a second and then jumped on the nearest pan.

"I'm going out," he shouted.

Pudloo gasped. Pudloo knew of the dangers. Palaya was not the first person who had slipped from an ice pan and drowned in the frigid waters. Jimmy could slip off himself. Even if he reached Palaya in time, how would he get him out of the water with all his heavy, wet clothing? Jimmy was not big. If Palaya panicked and struggled he could pull Jimmy in with him.

These thoughts tumbled over each other through Pudloo's mind for only a second. Pudloo also knew Jimmy. He knew that if Jimmy didn't try he would live with a guilty feeling the rest of his life. Pudloo would not wish that on Jimmy.

"Take care," he called to Jimmy. Already Jimmy was well on his way to the sound. He jumped from one ice pan to another until he was on one close to Palaya. He crouched down and reached forward. He was not close enough. Palaya would struggle frantically for a moment and then lie quietly as he drifted into unconsciousness in the cold water. Palaya was unconscious now. In this condition he couldn't even reach out to Jimmy.

"Pudloo, throw me a sealing hook," Jimmy hollered.

Pudloo grabbed a sealing hook from shore, jumped to the large ice pan closest to Jimmy and holding the hook in his hand threw it with all his might. Trying to keep one eye on Palaya, Jimmy turned long enough to see the long handle coming through the air towards him. If he missed, the sealing hook would float away. It came closer. He was no good at catching balls but somehow *must* catch this. Even in the freezing cold his hands began to perspire. He held them out. The handle slipped between his fingers. He closed them tightly. He had it!

Jimmy knelt down. Palaya was quiet now. He hated these seconds of stillness. Was Palaya dead or just unconscious? Jimmy stretched away out with the hook. It caught! Only then did Jimmy realize the *terrible* weight of an unconscious person. Jimmy lay flat as possible on the ice and hooked his toes around the edge. Palaya was too heavy. The hook slipped loose.

Jimmy reached again.

"If I can hook him when he's fighting," Jimmy thought, "I might be able to save him. It's not going to be easy. He's heavy."

Palaya slipped past the hook.

Jimmy threw down the hook. Tears of anger and frustration prevented him seeing. Desperately he dashed them away with his sleeve.

Why had he come anyway? If he hadn't, no one would have blamed him. They hadn't expected a twelve year old to even try. But now that he had come — what about that? What if he couldn't possibly save Palaya? Would they blame him? How would he feel?

But he *had* come and whether Palaya lived or died depended on him alone.

"Alone!" In all his twelve years, even when he had first gone South to school, he had never felt so alone as he did now on the slippery ice pan in the freezing water of the Bay. He could see the people clearly on the shore, as much help to him as though they had been hundreds of miles across the tundra.

"Whether Palaya lives or dies depends on me." Jimmy picked up the sealing hook once again, lay flat on the ice and found the best foothold possible for his toes. Once again he reached out for Palaya. He was discouraged and losing hope. Jimmy reached as far as he dared. There was a jerk at the end of the hook. The sealing hook had snagged! It was lodged in part of Palaya's clothing. But had it caught firmly enough to hold against Palaya's struggling? Jimmy pulled to test the grip — gently at first and then a little harder. The hook held!

Jimmy began to pull Palaya towards the ice pan — slowly and carefully so as not to dislodge the hook. It was impossible to believe that Palaya could weigh so much. Jimmy's arms strained. Each muscle ached. His body was numbing from the cold ice. Still, through his anesthetized body he could feel the muscles in his groin stretch until he was sure they would snap with the weight of Palaya. And still he pulled. Palaya's body dragged toward the ice pan. As Palaya came closer, Jimmy lifted the hook to raise his head from the water. Palaya's head hung limply; no inner message compelled him to try to raise it from the water.

Jimmy looked around him. How small his ice pan was.

"I can't bring Palaya onto this pan. It will sink and we will both drown."

He looked down at the sagging head. He had to do something. Palaya might not be dead but if he wasn't he sure wasn't breathing very evenly. Through Jimmy's mind flashed the Life Saving Course he had taken in Scouts. Artificial respiration! That's what Palaya needed. But the course had been so long ago. Could he remember? With the hook he pulled Palaya as far out of the water as he safely could. When the ice pan began to tip he secured the handle of the hook tightly under his arm. He knelt on the cold ice and gently raised Palaya's head. Talking to himself as if commanding his memory to perform Jimmy said "Clear the mouth of anything . . . Tilt the head back . . . Squeeze the nose . . ." Slowly it all came back to him. When he had done all those things he began breathing into Palaya's mouth. Once, twice, three times. No response.

"It may not be exactly right, Palaya, but it's the best I can do. Please, Palaya?" Four, five, six times. Did Palaya take a breath or was it simply the wind in his clothing? Seven, eight. Yes! Yes, Palaya was breathing. Faintly — but by himself! Nine, ten, eleven times. It was growing stronger. Although it was not strong, Jimmy knew he could not leave him much longer in the cold water. He paddled towards shore where they could get Palaya to a warm place and to the village nurse. Surely someone on shore had gone for her. He paddled with his free hand. He paddled with all his strength. The ice pan moved so slowly, partly because he was tired and partly because of the drag of Palaya's body in the water. Jimmy dropped his legs into the water and tried to push with them as well. It was awkward holding the sealing hook with one hand and trying to paddle the ice pan. He could feel his strength leaving him. Turtle-like he moved toward shore. *The water was so cold!* Jimmy had no feeling now in his arms or legs but still he pushed back the water with them.

The adults watched silently as Jimmy came closer to shore. Was Palaya alive? They couldn't tell from where they stood. They could see that Jimmy's strength was lessening. Several of the men waded out to meet him. Gently they lifted Palaya from his icy bed. He lay very still but his breathing was more steady now. On the beach they wrapped Palaya in a skin robe and tucked another one tightly around Jimmy's shoulders as they headed for the Nursing Station.

"They will take care of Palaya now," thought Jimmy. "I am no longer alone." Suddenly, his legs felt like elastic bands. The robe seemed to weigh him down. For a moment he was sure he would have to sit down on the bench before he fell down.

Governor-General Vanier finished speaking with Jimmy, shook his hand and with a smile left the room. As his back disappeared through the door, Jimmy's legs felt exactly as they had that night on the beach. Elastic bands! He looked frantically around the room for a chair in case they gave out on him.

"Some hero I am," Jimmy thought. "I can't even make my own legs do what I want them to." He shrugged. "Yeh, a *real* hero!"

Survival
Eugene S. Hollman

We are on an Arctic flight with:

NELSON, *a mining engineer on his first trip to the Arctic.*
CARTER, *an elderly doctor on an emergency call to an Arctic village.*
ARVIK, *an Eskimo returning from two years in the service.*
STEVENS, *the pilot.*

NELSON   *It began one February day on a bush plane flying to Pelly Bay. There were three of us in the cabin — a Dr. Carter, myself, and a young Eskimo named Arvik. I had never been into the far north until the company sent me up to examine a property.*

CARTER   *(Talking over the noise of the motor.)* And in spite of what this young man has told you, Nelson — the Arctic is a nasty, brutal place.

ARVIK   To the white man, Dr. Carter. Not to my people.

CARTER   You've been away, Arvik. Your two years in the army will make it look different.

ARVIK   That may be so, Dr. Carter.

NELSON   Tell me, haven't the big new developments made a change — the mines, the new defense centers?

CARTER	Ah, yes! But that's different. The white man's Arctic is something else altogether. It's insulated, protected from the Eskimo's Arctic by the white man's in-ventiveness. His aim is to make the Arctic as much like New York or Montreal as he can — without women.
NELSON	(Laughing) And the natives on the outside looking in.
CARTER	As always.
ARVIK	We have our life. Away from the trading posts and the camps, many live in the old way.
NELSON	Hunting? Fishing?
ARVIK	Yes.
CARTER	And following old superstitions. Mind you, Nelson — I'm not an old Arctic hand. Can't be when I'm only up here on emergency cases. But the life I see in the native camps — well, it's no life for a human being. It's ignorant, brutal.
ARVIK	The land is hard — but I will be glad to see my people again.
CARTER	Ever seen a dog tied to a stake and killed with a whip, Nelson?
NELSON	No.
CARTER	I have. Whenever I dream of getting lost up here, that's what I see. (The engine coughs, then conks out.)
ARVIK	Listen!
CARTER	Wonder what's up. Are we landing?
NELSON	Doesn't sound like —
STEVENS	(Coming through the inter-com.) Fasten your belts! Get your belts on fast! I've got to make a wheels-up landing. The escape door's on your left under the red light. Hurry!
NELSON	Great heavens!
ARVIK	Roll a blanket in front of your face. If we crash it will save your head.

NELSON	At least the ice looks smooth.
ARVIK	No. It will be rough along the shore.
STEVENS	Coming in! Coming in! Get ready!
CARTER	Oh, Lord, I hope he makes it.
NELSON	Hold on! Hold on! Here we go!

(*There is a grating of the aircraft on the ice, a jolting crash. Then dead silence.*)

CARTER	Any bones I can set?

(*Arvik and Nelson can't help laughing.*)

NELSON	That wasn't as bad as I expected.
STEVENS	(*Opening the pilot's door and calling urgently.*) Let's get out of here! Quick!
CARTER	But, Captain Stevens, it's a little —
STEVENS	Get out! The left tank has split. There might be a fire. Grab what you can — blankets, clothes, parachutes, anything! But get out fast!

NELSON	*We jumped out into the blinding midday sun and ran. From a hundred yards away we lay in snow — afraid to watch and afraid not to. Great clouds of vapor hissed away from our mouths. I could feel the cold creeping into my body at the places where my clothing was thinnest. And then a red curl of flame reached the gasoline. A great explosion and a sudden redness!*
STEVENS	No, no, no, no!
CARTER	Easy, Stevens, easy.
NELSON	Put this blanket around him, Carter.
STEVENS	I couldn't even call base. Didn't have time, didn't have time.

NELSON	*A part of my mind kept repeating an old army phrase: Take stock of equipment. Equipment. I could feel the matches in my pocket and the chocolate bar I had bought at the PX in Churchill. Cigarettes. My pen and pencil. And otherwise just*

clothes — and a batch of magnetometer maps in my bag. I don't know what the others were thinking. We just lay there in our parkas, watching Arvik poking about in the smoking, twisted pieces of the plane.

ARVIK   Who wishes to hunt the shore for wood?

NELSON   It's just rock and snow. There isn't any wood.

ARVIK   Along the shore there will be driftwood, frozen, lying under the snow. There is always wood on this coast.

CARTER   I'll go.

ARVIK   Take Captain Stevens along with you, Doctor. Look for small drifts above the ice. Kick them. If you find wood, here is a bar from the plane's wing to pry it loose.

CARTER   Okay, okay.

ARVIK   Do not touch it with your skin — it will stick.

STEVENS   What are you going to do?

ARVIK   Mr. Nelson and I will make a snow house.

CARTER   Just like that?

ARVIK   There is nothing else. We cannot live in the open.

NELSON   Call me Jim when you feel like it.

ARVIK   Jim?

NELSON   Yeah, sure. Jim.

ARVIK   There are pieces of metal by the plane, Jim. They can make us two snow knives. Maybe they will build us a house before the sun goes.

NELSON   *(He and Arvik are hacking and slicing at the frozen snow.)* How long have we got, Arvik?

ARVIK   Long enough. We were lucky to find good snow so quickly.

NELSON   *I* was lucky. You knew where to look.

ARVIK   There are many kinds of snow — one good for the sled, one good for water, one good for building. Many, many kinds.

NELSON   Am I cutting it right now?

ARVIK   No, no, Jim, the block will break. Here: you slide the steel back and forth, deeper into the drift, a little

	longer to save time. Now, underneath. Yes, yes. That is a better one.
NELSON	I do one, you do ten. And *my* wrist aches.
ARVIK	It is not used to this. It is cold. Put your hands inside your parka while I place the blocks.
NELSON	I didn't know these things were built in a spiral.
ARVIK	What is a spiral?
NELSON	You're making one.
ARVIK	Oh?
NELSON	Sure. You just built the bottom row in a circle — then sliced it off in a sort of climbing curve.
ARVIK	Is that wrong to you?
NELSON	No, no. It's smart engineering. All you have to do is build around till you get to the top — one continuous row.
ARVIK	We have always done it like this. How are your hands now?
NELSON	I guess they're alive. They sting enough.
ARVIK	Good. Hand me the blocks that are cut.
NELSON	*In just over an hour Arvik built us an igloo, using the snow the cold had frozen — to keep out the cold. Without knowing geometry he constructed a perfect half-sphere, knowing the right shape to offer the wind the least resistance known to aerodynamics. The final block in the peak of the igloo was the same as the keystone any stonemason knows. And the door faced south to the sun.* *Carter and Stevens came back with one bleached timber between them, and Arvik took the wood into our igloo. After he had thawed one end of the timber he started chipping and whittling at it, singing monotonously.*
CARTER	For heaven's sake, can't you stop that whistling?
ARVIK	It is a song I learned in the Army, Dr. Carter. Perhaps it does not suit the work of chipping wood for a fire.

CARTER	Uh.
NELSON	Getting anywhere, Arvik?
ARVIK	The wood is still frozen. Where I have thawed it between my hands it is wet. The centre will be dry enough for a fire — if I can split it with the stone knife.
CARTER	What time is it, Stevens?
STEVENS	Six o'clock, by my luminous dial.
CARTER	They won't come now, will they?
STEVENS	No. There won't be any planes over.
CARTER	If it hadn't been for that blasted oil line of yours, Stevens —
STEVENS	It was a fluke, I tell you. Nobody can call those things.
CARTER	I know, I know, I know.
NELSON	We've lost our insulation, Carter.
CARTER	Eh? What do you mean?
NELSON	What you were saying a minute before the crash. This time the white man's inventiveness can't protect us from the Arctic.
ARVIK	Give me a match now. I have the wood ready.
NELSON	Here's two. That leaves forty-one to go, Arvik. Don't waste them. *(The precious match is scratched.)*
CARTER	Keep your fingers crossed.
ARVIK	Come, little chip of wood. Come, make a flame for us. Now I will fan you softly, softly.
NELSON	It's beginning to glow.
STEVENS	Blow on it. *(Stevens leans forward and blows.)* Blow on it, Arvik.
ARVIK	Stop! Stop it, Stevens!
STEVENS	I was just —
ARVIK	Now it is gone. You cannot blow a fire to life, Captain. Your breath is wet in this cold. A flame must be fanned with your mitt or a stick.
STEVENS	I'm sorry. I didn't know.
ARVIK	I will try again when it dries.

STEVENS	The mistakes you can make!
NELSON	Forget it, Stevens. Reminds me of a thing I read during the war: If you get lost in the jungle, remember the natives can teach you a lot. They've got the know-how of centuries right in their heads. They know *how* to live *where* they live. You don't.
STEVENS	Well, did you?
NELSON	Get lost, you mean?
STEVENS	Yeah.
NELSON	Twice. I read the survival manual from cover to cover. But I sure watched the natives.
CARTER	Tell me, how do they start fires?
NELSON	They were pretty smart about fires. In the jungle they use a piece of string and three sticks of wood.
STEVENS	How does it work?
NELSON	They use a wooden bow, perhaps a couple of feet long. By looping the string around a stick they can make it twirl every time the bow is moved back and forth.
STEVENS	Like a drill?
NELSON	That's right. You place one end of the drill in a notch in the wood you're trying to light, and saw like mad with the bow. Bow spins drill. Drill rubs wood. Fire burns wood.
STEVENS	Nothing to it, eh?
NELSON	I left out the hard part.
STEVENS	What's that?
NELSON	Cutting the notch you're drilling in. It's got to be shaped like a keyhole. Your drill works in the round part, but the tinder sits in the long end, barely touching the drill. You know, it took me two weeks to learn that?
CARTER	It's always easy — if you know how.
NELSON	They know how.
STEVENS	It really works, eh?
NELSON	Sure. It's just applied friction. That's the key to any

	number of fire makers: the drill; the fire thong; the plow.
CARTER	I still prefer a good match.
NELSON	And you light it with friction, Doctor. The natives like matches, too. But if you don't have them, you make fire with your hands — and with your head. First principles. The character who made the first match knew about fire before he started. And somebody told *him* what those first principles were.
CARTER	I never looked at it that way.
ARVIK	Give me the larger sticks, quickly. The flame is starting to catch.
NELSON	They're right there, Arvik, right beside you.
ARVIK	We must take care of this fire. We must not let it go out till our clothes are dry.
CARTER	You know, Nelson, somehow I feel I'm discovering fire for the first time.
NELSON	*(February the 6th. I began my journal that first night, writing clumsily with my mitts on — by the light of that precarious, spitting little fire Arvik had made for us. And long after I fell asleep I could hear Arvik, busy at something, pounding and tapping and pounding at some inscrutable piece of metal, humming an Eskimo song.)*
NELSON	How is it coming, Arvik? Almost through?
ARVIK	It is slow. The canvas bags of the parachutes do not care if we have cold feet. They do not want to become shoes — and they fight the knife I have made.
CARTER	Cigarette, Nelson?
NELSON	Thanks.
CARTER	Stevens?
STEVENS	Nope. *(Coughing.)* I get enough smoke from that fire!
NELSON	Anything wrong, Stevens?
STEVENS	Nope.

ARVIK	Many times I have seen my mother sewing the kamiks. She would frown at this canvas. But we have no skins to use.
CARTER	Do you need any more of my sutures?
ARVIK	No, Doctor. I have enough for the last one. *(Pause.)* Have you sewn many people with this needle, Dr. Carter?
CARTER	Quite a few.
ARVIK	You must have great skill to do that — inside a man's body.
CARTER	Takes a long time to learn.
ARVIK	Where does a man learn these things?
CARTER	We have special schools, Arvik. The same as you had in the Army — only they teach doctors. You watch others and read books and study.
ARVIK	I would like that.
CARTER	I can't make a shoe cover, Arvik.
ARVIK	Ha! My mother would laugh at these! "Did you not chew them, my son? Can a man keep his feet from turning to ice without furs? You are a senseless man to go away without skins or a woman to keep your clothes and light the fires."
NELSON	Woman — the indispensable tool. Anywhere.
ARVIK	Better than a knife! Better than blubber to fill the lamp! One can find a knife by splitting a rock. One can kill a seal.
CARTER	*(Sighs.)* Ah, me. *(Choking from the smoke.)*
NELSON	A penny, Doctor?
CARTER	Nothing at all, Nelson. Just that I'd always imagined myself as an old man, having something witty or wise to bring to a crisis. And I haven't.
NELSON	What is it the manual says? Survivors should sing, laugh, tell jokes. Keeps up the morale and time goes quicker.
CARTER	I can't think of a joke about starving.
STEVENS	Old Mother Hubbard went to the cupboard

To find her poor dog a bone.
But when she got there —
(Stevens begins to get shrill.)
Have some ice water, anybody! Nice fresh ice water!
Melted continuously in a tin can!

CARTER Shut up, Stevens.

STEVENS *(Mimicking him.)* Shut up, Stevens. Shut up, Stevens.

CARTER Be quiet!

STEVENS You be quiet! I'm too hungry. My stomach is in knots from drinking that stuff. So if I want to make a joke, I'll make a joke.

CARTER I'm twenty years older than you are, young man and I —

STEVENS You can starve at any age, old man.

CARTER Why, you —

NELSON Stop it! Cut it out, both of you!

STEVENS Who put you in charge of the party?

NELSON Nobody's in charge — you, me, or anybody else. We're in this together.

CARTER What is this, Nelson — Eskimo logic?

NELSON I don't care what you call it. All I know is we're sunk if we don't think, plan, work together — till we're out or till we're dead. I know that much from my time in the jungle.

CARTER I apologize, Stevens.

STEVENS Forget it. I'm sorry.

NELSON We're sorry, Arvik.

ARVIK It is because we cannot do anything. A storm which keeps men in the house for a long time, waiting, breeds a storm in the house, too. If the wind falls we must hunt tomorrow.

CARTER Hunt? With our bare hands?

ARVIK No. Perhaps I can make a harpoon.

NELSON What are we going to hunt for, Arvik?

ARVIK The sea contains fish, and the bearded seal waits

under the ice for a harpoon. The fox and wolf can be killed without guns. In my country a man can kill anything if he knows the way.

NELSON   *(February the 7th. About dusk the snow stopped. Arvik, Stevens, and I drove holes into the four-foot ice with a steel bar from the wreckage. Then we let down our lines, and (as Arvik would say it) the black salmon welcomed a hook that was nothing more than the key from an empty ration can, bent like a pin. Tomorrow we hike up the coast.)*

ARVIK   Nothing is alive. Nothing is stirring yet after the storm. Our feet are silent in the new snow.

CARTER   Did you ever see such a sight, Nelson? Look at that bay — not a mark, not even a ripple in the snow.

NELSON   Be happier if we saw some animal tracks somewhere. That's one thing you've got over the jungle boys, Arvik.

ARVIK   What is that, Jim?

NELSON   In the snow you can track your game inch by inch.

ARVIK   Yes.

NELSON   I've watched natives in the South Pacific follow a trail by the way the leaves were disturbed. You can't see a thing, but they get all excited over a broken twig or a flat piece of grass. "Monkey here! Monkey here!" Sure enough, there's a monkey around.

ARVIK   They must be men of great knowledge.

NELSON   They are.

ARVIK   I think there will be a river beyond that ridge. Look at the clouds over there.

STEVENS   Nothing special about them, Arvik. Strato-cumulus, two thousand feet.

ARVIK   Do you not see the pattern?

CARTER   What pattern?

NELSON   You mean that break where the sun's coming through?

ARVIK   Yes. The sky is sometimes a map of the land underneath. When a valley is seen above there is one below. Let us go there — we may find fresh-water ice. Maybe some live willow branches, too.

STEVENS I'll bet you five to one there's no river.

ARVIK   *(After a pause.)* I am wrong, Stevens. There is no river — only a deep cut into the land for a tongue of the sea.

STEVENS You won your money, Arvik.

NELSON   There are a few pieces of driftwood.

ARVIK   Driftwood and something else. See where the wind has blown the beach clear of snow — that is old ice. It will give us fresh water.

CARTER   How can you tell it's old?

ARVIK   Look at it. It is blue and it shines. When you strike it, it will break like glass.

NELSON   It all looks the same to me.

ARVIK   *(Laughing.)* Is it possible? New ice is gray, milky. But that is old ice over there. It has hid from the sun under that cliff for many seasons. Now that the salt is gone, the water will be sweet.

STEVENS Tell me, how did it get there?

ARVIK   Does someone ask why the sun is warm or the seas wet?

CARTER   Probably driven up by the wind, Stevens. I've seen pack ice jammed up at Pelly Bay in July.

ARVIK   I do not know. Maybe an *angiut* left it for us. The helping spirits know all about everyone.

NELSON   *(On February 9th and 10th, it stormed, and I wrote in my journal: "Arvik is a mixture of technician and mystic, like most men. What observation can teach, he knows. What doing can prove, he accepts. Without knowing physics, he observes the effect of adiabatic changes in the atmosphere, and correlates a break in the clouds with an unseen valley. What meteorologist could do better? And no meteorologist would spot the old sea ice — in spite of knowing that sublimation removes the salt with time. Without books, he preserves the past. And yet, he believes in spirits.*

"We have no food now. If it stops blowing tomorrow, Arvik and I will go after seals. He has made us two harpoons — shafts from driftwood, heads from the brass case of the plane's compass, lines from the nylon cords of the parachute. We will see.")

ARVIK   *(Walking with Nelson in the snow.)* There will be no caribou along the coast, Jim. When the sun goes away they follow it.

NELSON   You never keep caribou. Why?

ARVIK   What could we feed them — ice?

NELSON   Don't you ever think —

ARVIK   Wait! Let us be still. *(Pause.)* See the small rise in the snow. Something is coming up to breathe at a hole there. *(He runs through the snow.)* Quickly! Softly! *(Pause.)* Now! *(He plunges his harpoon into a pocket of water and ice.)*

NELSON   Did you get him?

ARVIK   It is too late. You have only one chance.

NELSON   It's the first hole we've found.

ARVIK   We are lucky. Now we know there are seals under this ice.

NELSON   It won't help if we don't get one.

ARVIK   You will stay here, Jim. I have scraped new snow over the hole which the seal has gnawed. The small stick is in place. If you see the stick move, drive the harpoon down with all your strength.

NELSON   *(I stood on the ice with my back to the wind, crouching over the hole. Arvik walked slowly in widening circles around me, probing the snow with a bent piece of wire — pausing, then going on. Then he stopped. He had found one. Time seemed to crawl as we watched the unmoving slivers of wood in the snow. It came to me that I was hunting for my life — directly — with nothing between me and this one objective. Knowing the shape of a mine shaft had no meaning in this environment, nor the sound of a Geiger counter. The hand and the spear and the eye held all the answers to survival.)*

ARVIK   Nelson! Nelson! We have one! Come and drink the hot blood of the seal! *(Long pause.)*

CAST   For he's a jolly good seal,
For he's a jolly good seal,
Which nobody can deny.
(Laughter.)

STEVENS   You know, Nelson, I thought you'd been stabbed. Your whole face was bloody.

ARVIK   He did not want to take it. I had to open his mouth, and then he choked!

NELSON   I never drank blood before. Almost scalded my face off.

ARVIK   You were cold from standing so long. That is why it was hot to your lips.

STEVENS   Do you think it has stewed long enough?

CARTER   Eat slowly, Stevens. It's going to be strong.

ARVIK   What will you eat first? A flipper? A piece of the lip?

STEVENS   Anything — anything.

ARVIK   Ah.

CARTER   For what we're about to receive, Lord, make us truly thankful. Amen.

STEVENS   Amen.

NELSON   Amen.

ARVIK   What is wrong? Does no one wish to eat?

NELSON   Grace before food, Arvik. It's a custom sometimes among us.

ARVIK   Like blowing sweet water into the seal's mouth. We do that so the dead seal will tell his brothers we gave him a drink. They live in the sea; they are always thirsty.

CARTER	Did you do it this time, Arvik?
ARVIK	Yes. On the ice, I melted snow in my mouth for the dead seal. His brothers will not avoid us.
CARTER	Amen.
STEVENS	Is it all right if we eat now?
ARVIK	Everything. Eat everything but the eyes. We must have them to keep evil spirits away if we travel to Pelly Bay.
NELSON	*(February the 12th. We have killed three seals now. Tomorrow we start for Pelly Bay dragging our gear on a sealskin sled. Arvik makes even the cold work for him. The runners are strips of sealskin well soaked with water and frozen rigid. We're going overland. Four men on the tundra. A hundred miles.)*
ARVIK	*(Shouting over a howling wind.)* We cannot stop here. To reach Pelly Bay with food we must not stop here.
NELSON	Carry on, Arvik.
ARVIK	Keep the slatted wood over your eyes, Stevens. Without sun, you can still go blind in the snow.
STEVENS	Okay, okay, okay!
CARTER	Can't something be done about the sled? It's getting heavier all the time.
NELSON	We're just tired, Carter.
STEVENS	You're crazy, Nelson. Feel it; it drags like a stone.
ARVIK	That will be the runners. We must renew the mud and the ice to make them run smoothly.
NELSON	It's a long way to water.
CARTER	Can't we stay here? Can't we build a shelter and melt snow?
ARVIK	Is that what is wanted?
CARTER	I'm tired. I'd like a rest. I'm an old man, Arvik.
NELSON	How far should we go, Arvik?
ARVIK	Five, maybe six, miles. We should do six miles before dark.

NELSON	We won't start again if we make shelter. Not before dark.
ARVIK	What is the wish of the others?
STEVENS	Fix the sled and I'll go.
NELSON	Carter — what about you?
CARTER	I'll go, if I have to. I'll go.
ARVIK	Take the mud bag from the sled. We will have to build a fire to get water.
NELSON	*(February the 19th. We have come sixty miles on the way, but the meat is running out. Carter is very tired. Arvik and I went searching for iron pyrites among the rocks. No luck. The fool's gold eludes us. But this fool stumbled into a crevice and twisted a knee. A painful reward for my ignorance of snow. Three matches left. Unless we find bits of pyrites, the blubber won't be much use. Forty miles to go.)*
STEVENS	Come on, Doc. On your feet. Sled's waiting for us.
CARTER	What day is it?
STEVENS	The same as yesterday; the same as tomorrow; forever and ever.
NELSON	It's the twentieth, Carter. We've been on the march eight days.
CARTER	Eight days — is that all?
NELSON	That's all.
CARTER	I'm not going, Nelson. I'm going to stay behind.
NELSON	Don't be crazy. You're coming if we have to carry you.
CARTER	Listen to me, Nelson, Stevens.
STEVENS	He's pretty bad. Ankles all swollen.
NELSON	We'll put you on the sled, Carter. We'll pull you. The three of us can manage.
CARTER	Ask Arvik to come here.
NELSON	He's fixing the sled.
CARTER	I want to see him.
STEVENS	I'll get him.

NELSON	Now let's take it easy, Doctor. Forty miles and we'll be in Pelly Bay.
CARTER	Don't try to confuse me, Nelson. And watch your knee. Or you'll be next.
ARVIK	What is it?
NELSON	He wants to see you.
ARVIK	Yes.
CARTER	You'll give me an honest answer, Arvik?
ARVIK	Yes.
CARTER	What chance is there of your getting through to Pelly Bay — with me on the sled?
ARVIK	It is not easy to say. We may find a cache — or kill a fox. Then we would all have new strength.
CARTER	Answer me.
ARVIK	*(Slowly.)* No. It is not likely.
CARTER	That's all I wanted to know.
NELSON	But, Carter.
CARTER	You heard him, didn't you? Now the three of you go like blazes for that Bay. If you make it — then you can learn how to live with your conscience. If you don't — what does it matter?
ARVIK	*(Pause.)* You are a good man, old man.
NELSON	What are you talking about? I'm not going to leave him here.
ARVIK	No, Jim, no. He speaks the wisdom of old men among my people. My own grandfather — not as old as the doctor but going blind — he left us one night for his long sleep on the ice. Without speaking. If the young and the strong ones are to live, the old and the weak ones must die. It is the way. . . .
NELSON	*(February 22nd. This may be the last entry in the journal of James Nelson, mining engineer. Arvik and Stevens have disappeared over the last ridge of ice. And my hope goes with them toward Pelly Bay. I am alone now, without food, with my knee in the*

*splints. I am afraid, and I keep a seal eye in my hand
— for safety. What life I have left or hope to have
again, I owe to Arvik — technician, mystic, man.)*

On Being Lost
Grey Owl

*"Grey Owl" was the name taken by a young Englishman,
Archie Belaney, who made his home in Canada. Fascinated by
the life of the Indian, and in love with nature in all its forms
and moods, he completely transformed his appearance and
ways of living and became known around the world as an
Indian trapper. His great ambition was to become the
protector of Canadian wildlife, and especially of "the beaver
people".*

Three years ago, on a night in spring, a man went down from
his camp fifty yards to the river to get a pail of water, and has
never been seen since.

A man may start on a bright, sunshiny day, with all
confidence, to make his way to some as yet undiscovered lake
or river, or to look over a section of country, and find his
trip going very satisfactory. Inviting glades, offering good
travelling, open up in every direction; gullies lead on
miraculously from one to another in just the right directions.

Having lured him in so far with fair promise, the fickle
landscape now decides to play one from the bottom of the deck.
The going becomes thicker during the next half-hour and the
ground inclined to be swampy, with quite a few mosquitoes
present. The interest aroused by these features induces a slight
relaxing of concentration, and during such a period of
preoccupation the sun guilefully seizes on this as the
psychological moment at which to disappear.

And on him dawns, with sickening certainty, the indisputable fact that he is lost. He becomes a little panicky for this begins to be serious.

He may be later stumbled upon, by the merest accident by some member of a search party, or by his partner, if the latter is a skilful tracker; or again, he may find his way to a large body of water and wait to be picked up by some Indian or other passer-by. This within a reasonable distance of civilization. If far in the woods, he will wander hopelessly on, sometimes in circles, at times within measureable distance of his camp, past spots with which he is familiar, but is no longer in a condition to recognize. The singing of the birds becomes a mockery in his cars; they, and everything around him, are carrying on as usual, each in his own accustomed manner of living, and yet he, the lord of creation, is the only creature present who is utterly and completely subjugated by his surroundings. Hunger gnaws his vitals, and hot waves of blood surge through his brain, leaving him weak and dizzy. Still he must keep on, always.

As he grows weaker he becomes the victim of hallucinations and is beset by a form of insanity, the "madness of the woods", in which the dim arches become peopled with flitting shapes and formless apparitions. Acquaintances stand beckoning in the same distance who, when he approaches, retreat yet further, and beckon again, finally fading to nothingness, or walking callously out of sight. And he shouts frenziedly that they may stop and wait for him, at which the woods become suddenly deserted, and his voice echoes hollowly through the endless, empty ramifications, which have now assumed the appearance of a tomb.

For another day, perhaps two, or even three, he stumbles on muttering, at times raving; falling, getting up, only to fall again; crawling at last in that restless urge of the lost to keep on while there is life; and always just ahead dangles the will-o'-the-wisp of hope, never fulfilled.

And if ever found, his bones will indicate his dying posture as that of a creeping man.

As late as four years ago I was guilty of a piece of bad judgment, or several of them, that left a considerable blot on my record, already none too spotless, and came near to settling for all time my earthly problems. The occasion was one on which it became necessary, owing to the destruction of a hunting ground by fire, to move several hundred miles to the north, and, in so doing, I failed to make the necessary allowance for changed climatic conditions. This resulted in my arriving behind season, and finding the trading post out of many things, and its stock, much depleted, consisting mainly of culled or damaged goods remaining after the Indians, now long departed for their hunting grounds, had taken their pick. Amongst these left-overs was a one and only pair of moose-hide mitts, too small to be of much use. Having at that time no hides of my own, I was obliged to take; the initial mistake, and one for which, later, I dearly paid.

There had been much softer weather after the preliminary cold snap, and I started out on on exploration trip on a wet, soggy day, on which dragging and lifting the slushed snowshoes was a heavy enough labour. I perspired profusely, and on leaving the chain of lakes on which my cabin was situated for the overland trip to other waters, I hung up my outside shirt and leggings and proceeded without them, a piece of foolishness bordering on the criminal.

All went well for the first few miles. The sky cleared, and it turned colder, which, whilst it froze my outer clothing, made it windproof, and lightened the heavy going considerably, the snow no longer clogging my snowshoes. The moon would rise shortly, and everything was coming my way. I anticipated an easy journey home; I had found beaver of a potential value amounting to some hundreds of dollars, and a little wetting damped my spirits not at all.

My outbound route had been very circuitous, and at a point

where I thought it would be to my advantage I attempted the old, oft-tried, and justly notorious expedient of a short-cut in the dark. On such a night, calm, clear and frosty, nothing could possibly go wrong, and I expected to strike my own tracks in a patch of timber near the lake where my clothing was, and so on home. Half an hour from that time, in my wet condition, I became chilled with the now rapidly increasing cold, and was again obliged to make fire in a small gully, where I waited the coming of the moon.

As the pale disc cleared the hills, the shadows shortened and I made out to see a small sluggish stream, picking its somnolent way amongst snow-covered hummocks of moss and scattered clumps of larches.

I examined the creek and having ascertained the direction of its flow, decided to go downstream, as long as its direction suited me; and turning my back on my sheltered nook, with its abundance of dry wood and friendly twinkling fire, I started on a very memorable journey.

The going was bad.

Presently the stream meandered off to the right, out of my projected line of travel, and the sides of the ravine fell away into low undulations, which flattened out and eventually disappeared altogether. I realized that I was on the borders of one of those immense muskegs with which this North Country abounds.

The moon, having become hazy whilst I was yet at the fire, was now circled by a band of rainbow hue, and before long became completely obscured; a storm threatened and soon became imminent. I cast behind me the last atom of discretion and pushed forward with all possible speed.

Bent almost double, gasping for breath, my clothing caked with frozen snow, becoming rapidly exhausted, I knew that, dressed as I was, I could not long survive in such a storm.

The insistent barrier of the wind became a menace, a tangible, vindictive influence bent on my destruction. All the power and spite of the hurricane seemed centred on my person with the intention of holding me back, delaying me until my numbed limbs refused further duty, driving me down, down in between the snow mounds, where, shrieking with triumph, it would overwhelm me with a whirling mass of white, and soon nothing would remain save the roar of the wind, the scurrying drift, and the endless, empty waste of snow.

How long this continued I do not know, but suffice it that in time I heard with certainty the roar of wind-tossed treetops, and soon a black wall of forest rose up before me, and I knew that I now had a fighting chance. I quickly skirted a section of the belt of evergreens, looking up in an endeavour to find a bare pole protruding through the black tops, indicating a dry tree, but could distinguish nothing. Entering the grove, I quickly chipped various trees, tasting the chips for dry wood; every one stuck to my lips, showing them to be green and impossible to start a fire with. A deadly fear entered my heart; supposing there was no dry wood, what then?

In a kind of panic I ran out into the open, and, the storm having abated somewhat, I saw, to my unspeakable relief, a tall dry tamarack standing no great distance away, and hidden from me till then.

I attacked it furiously with my axe, and now found that my wet mitts had frozen into such a shape that it was almost impossible to chop. I made several strokes, and the axe twisted in my grip and no more than dinged the tamarack, hardest of dry woods.

Once a glancing blow struck my foot, shearing through moccasin and blanket sock, drawing blood. Eventually the axe flew out of my numbed hands entirely and I lost precious seconds recovering it. There was only one alternative: I must chop barehanded. This I did, felling the tree, and continuing cutting it up until my fingers began to freeze. And then I found that my mitts, already too small, had so shrunken with the frost that now, hard as iron, I could not put them on again.

I marvelled somewhat that in this present day and age of achievement, with civilization at its peak, I should be beyond its help, dying in a way, and owing to conditions long supposed to be out of date. I got a slight "kick" out of the notion, and thus exhilarated, suddenly decided that this was no time and no place to die.

I laughed aloud, for I had a trump card; two of them, in fact, one up each sleeve; he should not freeze my hands, and so destroy me. I decided that I would freeze my hands myself. And so I did, butting and splitting, until my hands became bereft of power and feeling, fully believing that I had lost my fingers to save my life.

I made a fire. The agony of it as the circulation made its way through the seared flesh; and the fear of a horrible death by blood-poisoning, or a useless existence without hands! For a man finds these things hard to accept with the calmness expected of him, and I am perhaps of softer mould than some.

I later found that the muskeg skirted the lake, and the next morning as I moved out I discovered that the clump of spruce that I had originally intended to pass by was an offshoot of the forest that I was looking for, and that I had spent the night, half-frozen, within a rifle-shot of my discarded clothes.

So I am still in doubt as to whether that blizzard was intended to destroy me, or if it was not merely one of those rough but friendly attempts to set us on the right road, that we sometimes suffer at the hands of our friends.

Avalanche
Robert E. Gard

The Crow's Nest Pass, according to legend, received its name as a result of a great battle between the Indians of the Blackfoot Nation and the Crows. The scene of this battle was entirely obliterated by the greatest landslide ever known in the Rocky Mountains.

On the morning of April 29, 1903, a CPR westbound freight train crawled slowly through the Crow's Nest Pass, through the little mining town of Frank, and past the dim, massive shape of Turtle Mountain. The time was just after four o'clock.

To the boys on the train the trip was routine. The sounds were just the same: the dim, cold light was normal for the time of the year. In the caboose Sid Choquette, the brakeman, was thinking that he'd be glad when the sun came up, for the air was cold and damp.

In Frank the bartender at the hotel had just finished cleaning up. He'd had a hard night. He was going home to bed — just as soon as he got rid of a lone drunk who was hanging around. The barkeeper sighed, put on his hat and reached out his hand for the drunk's collar.

Down the street, Sam Ennes stirred in his bed. For some reason he was uneasy — he couldn't sleep. He struck a match and looked at his watch. The time was seven minutes past four. He lay down again, pulled the bedclothes over his shoulders. He shut his eyes, but in a minute he flicked them open again and lay there in the darkness. He strained his ears to hear the breathing of his wife. From another room, one of his daughters coughed.

In the Frank coal mine the night shift was getting ready to lay off. The nineteen men were tired, dirty, ready to quit. They plodded toward the mine entrance. One of the men noticed that the mine horses were acting very nervous. He was too tired to care.

In the Leitch household, the baby was crying.

At ten minutes past four hell broke loose in Frank. The whole top and north side of Turtle Mountain slid with a terrifying roar directly into the Crow's Nest.

The freight had just passed the mountain when the avalanche struck. The startled crew, looking back as the train bumped to a halt, heard a sound louder than the loudest thunder and saw what they thought was a heavy gas or fog rising from mountain and town. To their surprised eyes, the town of Frank seemed to have completely disappeared. The crew gathered at the rear of the train, huddled together silent, awed by the sudden tragedy.

It was Sid Choquette, the brakeman, who first remembered the *Spokane Flyer*. The express was shortly due to speed through the Pass on its way to the coast. The men could guess, as they looked back, that the CPR tracks lay covered by stone many feet deep.

There was only one thing to do, and Sid did that thing. He started back toward Frank, over the slide with pieces of rock still hurtling down from the mountain. The dust was so thick that he couldn't see what lay ahead. Some of the stones were as large as boxcars, but Sid went right ahead. He arrived in time to flag the *Flyer*.

Sam Ennes, who couldn't sleep, suddenly found himself pinned under the jagged timbers of his home. Desperately Sam pushed at the weight that held him down. After a terrible struggle he got free. His legs were torn by the nails in the boards. His face was bleeding from many cuts.

Somewhere he could hear his children crying.

He began frantically to search in the ruins. He found the three girls first, then his wife. They had miraculously escaped serious injury.

Suddenly Mrs. Ennes began to shriek that the baby, Gladys, was missing. They searched in the dust-filled darkness, and then Mrs. Ennes found the baby buried in slime and mud. Believing that the child was dead, Mrs. Ennes stumbled toward the faint light in the Maclean house beyond the stricken area. When she arrived, she discovered that the baby was alive and not even scratched. Mrs. Ennes herself had a broken collar bone.

In the mine the workmen reached the entrance. They found it blocked up tight. Believing that it was just a small cave-in, the men turned and went west to another smaller exit. The horses remained in the mine.

When the miners finally got outside, many of them knew

they would never see their homes and families again. A number of the houses were buried over 100 feet deep.

In the Leitch house three children escaped, while three others and the parents were killed. One of the children, a baby, was completely unharmed. It was found on a huge rock that had been pushed quite a distance along by the slide.

The unharmed people of Frank wondered what had brought the catastrophe upon them. Some said it was a volcano, others that it was an earthquake. Many thought it was a mine explosion or a great quantity of gas suddenly released.

That the side of Turtle Mountain, which seemed so friendly and protective, had simply slid down on the little town crouching under its shoulder did not occur to many, those first few hours. Tales of a visitation for sin were heard, and to the drunk leaving the barroom this seemed likely. He started to run — no one knew where.

Help was rushed to Frank — not that there was much anyone could do. The dead were already buried. The living were in mortal terror that the rest of the mountain would come smashing down.

Many of the passengers on the westbound train held up by the slide tried to walk across to the train waiting on the other side. They found their shoes cut to pieces, their clothing ruined in the limestone dust. *A Calgary Herald* reporter on the scene wired his paper: "To traverse two miles of boulders, some bigger than a railway coach, tossed into piles and ravines, is a task that tries a strong man, well shod. For people with thin shoes, unaccustomed to mountains, the trip is almost suicide. I had a suit of clothes ruined by the white lime, my boots were cut to pieces, and my physical system is a wreck that calls for at least a week's recuperation. Editor please note."

The slide occurred on Wednesday morning. On Saturday Frank was a deserted village. A committee, including the mine inspector, crawled up the side of Turtle and reported that they had seen large cracks, newly formed, which led them to believe that the slide would reoccur. This report, backed up by the statements of Engineer McHenry of the CPR that he had kept a careful watch on Turtle Mountain for most of a day and had seen the mountain creeping, convinced the remaining citizens of Frank that they should vacate. Most of them went to Blairmore.

For nine days a careful watch was kept. At the end of nine days, when no further general slide had occurred, Premier Haultain decided the citizens of Frank could return if they so wished. Many did return to live most of the summer in terror. Finally there was a smaller slide in September. The slide, according to the Calgary Herald, was never really reported. The Frank citizens feared the report would "damage the town commercially".

One of the touching incidents connected with the story concerns the horses imprisoned in the mine. All but two of the men escaped fairly easily, but all of the horses stayed in the mine.

When the rescue party managed to clear the main slope, some twenty-nine days later, they encountered a depressing sight. All but one of the horses had died of starvation and thirst. The animals had gnawed the mine props and the wood on the cars in search of food.

The remaining horse was fastened between a car and the side of the entrance. He was very weak — almost gone. The horse was given a few drops of water and brandy. He lifted his head. The party left in search of blankets to keep the horse warm since they could not move him. As they went they heard the horse neigh faintly several times. When they returned ten minutes later, the horse was dead. Old-timers say the horse died of a broken heart. He thought he was being left alone in the mine.

The greatest slide in the Rocky Mountains was the result of a combination of causes. There had been a mild earthquake in the region in 1901 which may have been a factor. The fact that large chambers had been opened up in the mine was thought by some to have caused the disaster.

Turtle Mountain, however, is peculiar. It is of limestone, overthrust upon shale, sandstone, and coal beds. The whole thing is an unusually weak mass of rock. There is some reason for believing that the slide can happen again, but Frank folk, apparently, are not worrying.

Most of the eighty persons killed that terrible morning were buried at the moment of death. Some were not, and they lie near Frank, with the following inscription on a common stone:

> Here Lie the Remains of Some of
> the Victims of the Frank Slide
> April 29, 1903

The Frank slide has become a tragic legend of the Canadian Rockies.

Disaster at Avalanche Mountain
Cecil Clark

It was just about 11:30 on Friday night, March 4, 1910, that CPR roadmaster Johnny Anderson hung up the phone in a tiny watchman's cabin 500 yards from snowshed 17 at the 4300-foot level in Rogers Pass, high in the snowbound Selkirk mountains.

Anderson had been phoning Revelstoke, 45 miles away, to advise chief dispatcher Charlie Cotterell that work on the nearby snowslide would have the track clear in a couple of hours.

Since dusk, Anderson's 63-man crew had been digging through the slide in blizzard conditions and an hour before midnight their steady, back-breaking efforts had resulted in a steep, 20-foot-deep cutting through the obstructing snow. On the track, back of the toiling gang, was a rotary plough, its headlight stabbing the snow-laden gloom. Behind it stood a locomotive, old 1657, a 1,600-class coal-burner, breathing wisps of steam against the snow-laden air.

Nearby, on a spur, were the three or four work cars that had brought the crew to the scene.

Now and again during the evening the plough had been used, pushed into the snowbank by the locomotive, then withdrawn when its blades encountered uprooted trees or rocks. True, there were spare blades on hand and a mechanic to fit them, but repairs were time-wasting. It had been mostly shovel work.

Of one thing everyone was sure, never before had they seen such a snowfall in the passes of the Selkirks. It had been snowing for a week now, and looked as if it would go on forever. Seven feet had fallen in nine days, a fall that would undoubtedly boost the winter average for this region. And the winter average was a whopping 33 feet!

Anderson, lantern in hand, left the watchman's shack, his head bent against the icy wind, and as he approached the slide and his eyes grew accustomed to the dark, he suddenly realized that the work gang was working without lights. Gone was the tell-tale flicker of their lanterns, gone also the illuminating beam of the rotary's headlight. Then, as he shielded his eyes to stare down the track, it occurred to him that also missing was the reflected red glare from the firebox of 1657.

Wondering a little as he floundered another 100 yards through the snow, suddenly he stopped as he was gripped by the import of an awesome discovery.

The locomotive was gone!

So was the rotary.

And so were the 60-odd snow-shovellers.

Along the track in their places were the giant hummocks of fresh snow, dotted here and there with protruding, uprooted trees and branches.

While he was telephoning an avalanche had come down and buried them all!

Maybe it was the noise of the wind outside the cabin, or the fact that the door was closed, that prevented him from hearing the rumble of disaster.

It was not till daylight that he got the full picture. The flanking edge of a 600-foot-wide snow mass had swept down the mountain to engulf the crew. But as Anderson stood in the dark, shaken by the wholesale tragedy, he heard a faint but undeniable cry for help that seemed to come from the broken timbers of the snowshed on the parallel track.

Plowing knee-deep through fresh snow in the direction of the sound, finally by lantern light he caught a glimpse of clothing in the snow close to the snowshed. It was fireman Bill Le Chance whom he freed, who groaned with pain because of two broken legs.

Making him as comfortable as possible, Anderson trudged back to the cabin to grab the phone and tell Cotterell of the biggest single mishap in the mountains since the railroad was built 24 years before.

For the next half-hour Anderson was busy, and in his probing around the scene, found four more survivors. One was the cook on the work train, who had a remarkable escape from death when the work cars were overturned.

With daylight the locomotive was found, derailed and under a bank of snow. Pinned underneath it was the dead engineer, W. J. Phillips. The snow plough was on its side, partly under the locomotive.

When Anderson's terse message hit the railroad division town of Revelstoke, the midnight clanging of the town's fire bell was first warning that an extraordinary emergency required full civic action. Divisional superintendent, Tom Kilpatrick was soon busying himself with a series of rapid-fire orders, and from the despatcher's office spare crews were alerted by phone, the messages carrying the railroader's top priority, SAP ("soon as possible"), guaranteed to make men leap from their beds, and grab their clothes. Soon, here and there, men were hustling through the snow-covered streets, buttoning mackinaws as they ran. To a railroader, nothing stands in the way of an SAP.

At the station, crews found that a train had been quickly made up, and blankets and medical supplies were being tossed aboard.

Being centre of the mountain division (Kamloops to Field), Revelstoke had a railroad-minded population, and close to one hundred volunteers arrived in the yards with their own shovels in case they were needed.

To get a proper appreciation of the mountain division's annual "men against the snow" problem, you first take a glance at what is undoubtedly one of the world's most stupendous pieces of railroad engineering. From Revelstoke the CPR tracks wind eastward and upward to climb and spiral and climb again over the Selkirks, which, back in those days, meant the summit of Rogers Pass. "Railroading on the roof of the world" it's been styled, for no tracks in North America go higher than these. Half a century ago (before the Connaught Tunnel was built) when the melodic wail of chime whistles on coal-burning locomotives resounded through these mountain gorges, as many as two, three and often four, 5,900-type locomotives pulled 4,000-ton trains at a panting 10 miles an hour up the "big hill", that spirals between Field and Yoho.

In winter it was here in high altitudes that the snowfall called for a continual patrol by snow ploughs from Revelstoke up through Rogers Pass, a lift of 2,400 feet.

For comparison, just imagine an E & N train leaving Victoria (if Victoria was 1,900 feet above sea level), and after climbing twice the height of the Malahat, arriving at Duncan near timber line, 4,300 feet above sea level. The analogy, however, doesn't tell half the story; in between, the train would skirt fantastic chasms and gorges, rumble over spidery bridges (the one at Stoney Creek is higher than a 25-storey skyscraper) and skirt a bare ledge around one mountain (Sir Donald) where the rock rises a sheer 1,000 feet beside the train.

East of Rogers Pass you could meet yourself coming and going through a series of extraordinary figure eights and spirals, that not only took you under a mountain but took your breath away at the same time!

It was up here in these mountain valleys that the hazard of snowslides, especially in Rogers Pass, accounted for the construction of five miles of snowsheds. Curiously enough, where snowshed 17 lay, on the north side of Avalanche Mountain, there hadn't been a snowslide reported since the road was built.

What starts a snowslide? Very little. Sometimes the reverberation of a passing train, the staccato bark from the stack of a hard-pulling locomotive can trigger a slide. Sometimes, under some jutting crag, small stones released by the noon-day warmth of a winter sun, bounce down a snow-laden slope to start a chain reaction. From small beginnings these slides gain power and momentum, and when the fluffy-looking mass starts turning over and over, it's a force beyond recall. If it encounters a rocky outcrop, the white, surf-like mass shoots in ski-jump fashion, over the top to spread like a fan and form an even wider front. Finally, interlaced with rocks and uprooted trees, the icy juggernaut comes to rest in a frozen river bed. Snowsheds are the safety factor for trains.

With every rampaging slide, comes a freak hurricane-force wind which can whip a man up and toss him through the air. It was such a wind that sucked fireman Bill Le Chance right out of the locomotive's cab and dropped him 60 feet away!

On the afternoon of the fateful March 4, 1910, eastbound passenger train No. 96 had been halted at Glacier and westbound 97 was 25 miles east of Rogers Pass. Passengers on 97 had a narrow escape, for as the engineer spotted a torrent of snow rumbling down the mountain, he cracked open the throttle to win a hair-raising, downhill race against the deadly menace of thousands of tons of snow. He made it by a mere hundred yards! Some said less, and pointed to the observation car platform loaded with snow!

By daylight, a work train from Revelstoke had arrived at snowshed 17, and scores of men started digging out the victims.

For an eye-witness account of what it was like, let's listen now to one who was there, 73-year-old Joe Godfrey who lives here in Victoria. Joe racked up a total of 50 years' service in the mountain division and was in that first gang dispatched to Rogers Pass.

"I was in Dan McEachern's bridge crew in those days," he told me, "and we'd come to Revelstoke just after midnight, after checking the Illicillewaet Bridge.

"As soon as we got in the yard," said Joe, "the despatcher had orders for us to pull right out. Someone said a bunch of men had been buried at snowshed 17."

From Joe Godfrey's word picture of events, it's easy to imagine the grim apprehension that gripped Revelstoke's 3,500 citizens that night.

By the time Joe Godfrey's rescue crew arrived and started digging, came word of another slide at shed 14 that had taken out 200 feet of track.

Where the ill-fated work crew was buried, Joe told me the snow was about 30 feet deep. Here again, it was a matter of slow hand-shovelling, for the rotary's blades would have cut into buried victims. All that Saturday and Sunday they shovelled snow and brought out dead men.

"We had a toboggan with us," he said, "and when we found a body we'd lower it down into the cut and bring him up.

"They never knew what struck them," he went on, "and I guess the noise around them, the howling of the wind, maybe prevented them from hearing the slide come down. They said at the inquest that there should have been lookouts posted."

There was deprecation in his tone as he added, "Lookouts wouldn't have made any difference. Nobody could have given warning in time."

He told me how they found four of the men in Dave Swannie's crew, who'd been digging in the cut and who apparently tried to run for safety.

"One of them must have tripped on a root in the snow," the veteran railroader recalled, "and when he went down three others fell on top of him. That's the way we found them, deep down in the snow.

"Most of those we dug out," he related, "were standing up. We found three foremen standing facing one another as if they'd been chatting. One even had his pipe in his hand. Another fellow, a Japanese, had his left leg bent, still standing up, as if he'd taken the first step to climb up. Another Japanese we found still had a cigarette paper clutched in his fingers. Just about to roll a smoke.

"Another work train full of volunteers left Golden that Saturday afternoon," said Joe, "but it only got to snowshed 14, three miles west of Bear Creek. From there they walked a mile and a half in the blizzard to lend us a hand."

There were other stories that eye-witness Godfrey told me — stories of bravery, of endurance and pathos.

There was the story about the engineer on the ill-fated plough, R. J. Buckley, who had been separated from his wife in Sarnia for 15 years and had just arranged a reunion. All set to leave for the east on Monday, his pass was there at the office alright, but Buckley had already gone on a longer journey.

Foreman J. Wellander, whom they dug up, had only been married a week. Back from his honeymoon that morning, he was dead by midnight.

Adrian Lathbury had an unusual experience, when he outwitted death for the third time in as many years. A track watchman, Adrian had the lonely job of patrolling the higher levels of the pass. He lived in a tiny cabin built of 12 by 12 snowshed timbers, his only companion a black and white border collie. Between trains, the only sign of life in the sub-alpine landscape was watchman Lathbury and his faithful dog.

A few days after the Avalanche Mountain disaster, Lathbury was patrolling the track near Bear Creek when there was an ominous rumble from above. When he turned to look he saw what seemed like the whole mountainside on the move!

In a matter of seconds the wind of the avalanche lifted him 15 feet in the air, whirled him over an embankment and plunged him in the deep snow on top of a snowshed 50 feet away. There he lay buried five feet deep, unable to move.

When Joe Godfrey and his fellow shovellers tackled this new slide eight hours later, they noticed a black and white dog furiously digging here and there in the snow.

"What's the dog digging for?" someone asked.

"Why that's Lathbury's dog!" said another, and following the animal's cue, half a dozen men started plying shovels until finally they got down to the watchman.

"He was face down, packed tight," Joe Godfrey told me. "So tight we even had to dig around his ankles and feet before we could lift him."

"Dead, I suppose?"

"No, he was breathing, and in a little while he was okay. He told us afterwards that he had a sort of detached feeling about the whole thing. He said it seemed as if he was watching someone else lying in the snow. He was uninjured and only complained of a stomach-ache where the snow had squeezed him too tight. If it hadn't been for his dog we might have missed him altogether.

"As a matter of fact," he went on, "the boys made quite a fuss about the dog, and later in the day while we were still shovelling, it got up on the pilot of the rotary, watching the proceedings. In those days we used to get the fan blades turning fast, then push the plough into the snow until the fan slowed up. Then the locomotive backed it up, and you repeated the trick. That is, when you didn't have rocks and stumps to contend with.

"Anyway," the ex-railroader continued, "this time the plough got pushed into the snow, and when the engine pulled it out somebody noticed the dog was gone. Somebody quickly figured it was stuck in the snow!

"Boy, was there a rush to dig him out! Got him out, too, none the worse. When he ran around among us, shaking out the snow and wagging his tail, someone cracked, "Like his owner . . . snow-proof!"

"He was proof against something, that Lathbury," said Joe with a grin. "Two or three years before he fell off a trestle into a swamp and nearly suffocated in the slime and mud before they dragged him out.

"A year later he fell off a freight and had his arm amputated. That's when they gave him the job of watchman on the snowsheds."

"Ordinarily, how much time does it take to get up steam for these sudden emergencies," was a question that occurred to me.

"In Revelstoke, no time at all," was Joe's reply. "Two locomotives are always standing by with steam up, one facing east, the other pointed west. All you need," he went on, "are the crews and an SAP from the office brings them on the run. When they get to the yard the train is already made up, the cook car attached, tools ready — everything."

Reminiscing about his early railroading days, Joe Godfrey told me he got two bits an hour when he first worked on a bridge gang.

Then he was wiper, later fireman ("We got $3 a hundred miles then . . . guess they get about $20 now"), and for 10 years before his retirement, he was a freight engineer.

When he worked on very early day snow ploughs, he told

me, two men handled the bar that lifted the plough blade, and another couple of men wound the wheel that operated the wings. And, of course, there were an engineer and fireman. Now the job's cut down to two men.

I glimpsed the "tricks in all trades" angle as Joe told of hauling 120 box cars out of Kamloops for Monte Creek, and the problems that attend performances like this. On occasion he has snaked 90 of them into Revelstoke, which is the limit for this stretch. Tricky work, too, for it takes all of five minutes for the air to reach the brakes on the extreme rear-end section; which means that as the front section is slowing up, the rear end is pushing you forward.

Joe Godfrey, born in Ware, in Hertfordshire, was a cabinetmaker by trade when he hit Revelstoke in 1909. He soon found that in the mountain vision there was more interest in bridges than bookcases or bureaus, so he went on the bridge gang.

He and his good wife, Amy (London-born and bred), have been married 47 years, and it was just a couple of years ago they forsook the Revelstoke mountains to make their home at 448 Superior Street. They have three boys, Richard (in Victoria), Douglas in Rossland, and Howard in Calgary. Howard has taken up where the old man left off; he's a diesel mechanic with the CPR at Calgary, a job that carries a hint of the vast changes that have taken place in western railroading since his father first climbed into the cab. Changes, by the way, that have also done away with most of the hazard of snowslides in the Selkirks. These have been minimized by the construction (1913-16) of the five-mile-long Connaught Tunnel (longest on the continent), which not only drops the railroad 550 feet below the previous summit level but also saves four miles of tracks and snowsheds.

It took $2,500,000 worth of dynamite to bore this $10,000,000 tunnel clear through Mount McDonald. With its completion, trains no longer ran the winter-time gauntlet of

Rogers Pass, and it's been a long time now since any trainman viewed with apprehension the snow-laden slopes of Avalanche Mountain.

The Agony of Mrs. Stone

Jon Whyte

Part One
1: Sunday, July 17, 1921

A statement isolated
between a question it poses
a question unanswered —

how she endured seven days
on the mountain

Her husband fell
from the summit of Eon
into death's isolation

"I can see nothing higher"
he had shouted
from the mountain's height
then fell

The rope

She sees him falling past her
waits for
braces for his weight

sees him fall

The body falls from ledge to ledge
dropping from sight in slowest motion
until it seems "it must have gone . . .
to the bottom of the mountain side . . ."

Stillness and isolation

Between the heavens and the earth
sun sets on the first day

2: Monday, July 18, 1921

Cautiously
she coils the rope
in the dawn

Dawn
clinging the summit
has not declined to the valley

No warmth of red glows in the cloudless dawn
Hot and pale it will be

Never so alone

Silver water trickles on a far mountain's face
Black forest waking beneath grey mountains

Descent alone

He had unroped
He had seen nothing higher
His ice axe held in his hand as he fell

Thirsty

She is very thirsty

Snow lies below on the mountain's steep south slope

Slight warmth in the sun

Stares into the chimney's gape
up which he'd scrambled

She had never climbed alone

By sunset of her first long day
she made her way by crumbling rock
to a ledge above the lower ledges

Climbing down is moving on a point
letting the mountain ascend
How strange
not to have noticed it

Delayed in searching for his body
she hoped might still have life
she bivouaced above the lower ledges
when darkness came

3: Tuesday, July 19, 1921

Must have slept
she could not remember sleeping
She had no dreams

Her elbows jostle her ribs
She distends a yawn to cease her teeth's chattering

Hears, she thinks, water trickling

On the infirm rock in the warming day
descends

They expected us yesterday
When we're not back today, they'll come looking
I'll meet them

By a rock tower she mistakes their route
taking a lower ledge narrowing to sheer cliff
retraces her steps ascending
sees a scree slope
beneath a chimney
seemingly descending
to the trees

By the ledge below

It is safe
leads a hundred feet to the slope
then the scree to the trees and camp

Warm again, her thirst slaked

Winds herself into the rope
turns her face to the wall
tests a rock; it is solid
fixes the rope
leans back
out down into the chimney

The ledge nears
The rope shortens
She is at the end of it
The ledge so close
She dangles at the rope's end
then drops the last ten feet

The rope swings above her
No need of it
She walks the ledge
feels its broad, level assurance
relieved to walk on its flat

The ledge narrows

A rock rattles loose and chatters away

She holds to the wall

The ledge is narrow now, too narrow

The scree slope seems so near

She edges her way back
explores the other end of the ledge

Thirsty

The ledge is closed

Nor up, nor down, nor off

The rope swinging above her
She cannot reach it
Tries to build a ramp of rocks but they are scant
She cannot reach it

The scree slope is near but she lacks the skill, the strength
lacks the rope

She takes her handkerchief from her pocket

Cannot cry

In a cleft a droplet of water

Jams the cotton into the crack
watches the handkerchief darken with the stain of damp

Today they are expected back

She winds her watch
times the hours it takes for her hanky to dampen for one sweet
quench
Curls her head between her knees
sleeps
Easier to sleep in the sun
stay awake the night

4: Wednesday, July 20, 1921

Today they will come
Anticipated yesterday at the latest
failing to arrive
we'll . . . I'll be looked for today
Today they'll send someone

Four hours for the drops to drench the hanky
three more at the most

Her stomach knots

Thinks about him rarely
thinks about water
their arrival
remembers the moss
how she put stale lips to it
could not draw its water out

126   Man *vs* Environment

Takes the cap from her watch
presses it into the moss
all her strength

It fills
The pressed moss yields its water
She drinks the capful, tries again
Only a few more drops

Soon they will be coming

Her throat must be wet enough to shout
Must not be greedy and force the moss dry

Bleak bands of cloud turn apricot, crimson, purple-black
as the light dies

5: Thursday, July 21, 1921

They made their way to the mountain yesterday
arrived at dark
They are up at the first light
beginning the search

She hears them moving in the darkness
tries to shout
but her dry throat
rattles a raven's croak
and she wakes
to the dark chill
can neither sleep nor stay awake

The sky lightens

She sees dawn inch down the slope
sees a flood of light
hears water fall to far away Gloria

In the sun's warmth she uncurls and lies in it

She must get up. She must walk. She must if . . .

She has strength; keep her muscles moving
make the rescue easier when
if they come

be ready to help

when they come

listen

The shade comes

The seeping water does not suffice

They do not come

They came
she thinks

came while she slept
she had not heard them

6: Friday, July 22, 1921

The days become nights
The ledge becomes a wall
that she is falling from
the nights days
and waiting action
She cannot stay awake
and stays awake
hears voices always

A spider wobbles over pebbles
spins a web of gossamer
between two rocks
Waits for flies to become trapped

They had come
found nothing
looked
shouted

and she had thought them dream

Why do they not come?

A mountain is too huge

She hears the cries of birds
The forest is not so far below that birds are alien

Puffed eyes, burnt arms, stiff and thickening fingers
No longer thinks about thinking
his death

Thinks about the water bottle in his pack

Things become more important than thoughts

Hears voices
a calling
hears a ringing
raises her head, leaning it drowsily listening

Hears nothing

Waste no hopes and thoughts on fantasies

Water and peace
the clear reflection in the still lake

Her lips drink the damp now before her mouth

Her pores call out
Tries with numb fingers to scrape the cheating dust from her
lips
Her pores call out

Drop by drop falling away from her

She would have a storm
snow and ice for their water
fountains to walk among
soft lush wet grass
tears
breakers

the pockmarks of water drops in dust

The shrivelling

The rope hangs above her

She lies on her back
stares at it

Night falls

7: Saturday, July 23, 1921

The spider caught and killed a fly
encasing it in silk

Go away, death, this ledge is too narrow

I knew you would come
You won't deceive me easily

or are you here to give me consolation?

Despair came with you

words wheeling
trying to keep in motion
the sphere of silence you'd impose

The exhilarating dizziness

We become smaller

a sense of looking up

mountain's visitors

gradually unfolding

Damn you, let me sleep

distended veins in the cold hands

Now my finger traces in the air as on a map the route

"nothing higher..."

stillness and isolation

earth, air, fire

where's water?

essentials

Deepset eyes glowing red with blood

Silence frames

permanence in ice

The marmots whistle on the scree below
If marmots whistle, there's reason for alarm

"Nothing higher..."

Nothing

8: Sunday, July 24, 1921

Slowly the light blurs her dry eyes in smears

She does not know time

Her swelled tongue
her scratched fingers do not heal

A scrabble of pebbles falls near her
She dares not move
Must pull herself to the edge to peer

She waits for the quilt of darkness

Death descends
not like the hawk or eagle plunging
but crawling upon her gently like the spider

The frail filament holding her will sever

She will lose her weight and his
like a loose web float on the rising air
swoop, waft, plume, and plummet

It flares, the candle sputters
the phoenix in the flame rises

the maples of autumn burning brightest
The white light on the gray rock blanches its features
They came and have gone
The light is darkness
and hope is despair
The mountain is a pit she must climb up from
Ecstasy a furrow
A stain upon the rock
my substance is my spirit
Soft voices at a garden party
Ice is clinking in the lemonade
It's so hot in Indiana in July
we should be in the mountains
Ah, our happy home, the tabernacled sky
umbrellas, parasols, clouds
a breeze from the river cools
Which day is it how long has it been celebrate the living
Serene here in the garden until it happens
I wish the autos didn't backfire so, scares the horses
why must the screen door slam
cannon at dusk   the lowering flag   seems   so beautiful
against the sky   it's fading
They've gone   against the sky
She shouts
hears a shout, a shot, echoing and subsiding
draws from the cleft the hanky
sucks it
Shouts again
hears a shout, shot, echoing and subsiding
Out of the dusk
from above

on a rope
in the long dusk of summer
Rudolf
descending

"Rudolf," she whispers, "I knew you would come..."

Then she sleeps

Part Two

Margaret Stone is the questions she has become

Photographs of her in albums almost reveal a face
shadowed as it is by wide-brimmed hats
underexposed, at distances too great for detail
in darkness against white snow, in profile against the sky

In the shadow of her husband's death
and in the shadow of her long days and nights
she persists in the meagre knowledge
we have of her
endures perenially the ledge she endured a week
the ledge she still endures in memory
collapsing on Eon's rotten rock
an echelon of questions

Still night stars' slow rotating
space, night, days, ledge, life—
the rope in the chimney above the bleak, grey rock to the
mountain's top
and the rope in the chimney above the ledge of her endurance
curl into question marks
to questions that cannot be answered—

When you pieced your shattering together
what pieces were you missing?

What was your face before time chiselled it?
Always in shadow?

The Agony of Mrs. Stone   133

Beyond the smoke and in the shade
Mount Eon in the backdrop
reclining almost visible
Margaret Stone in the last photograph taken by her husband

She persisted
She endured these things:

> reduction
> solitude
> pain
> thirst
> cold
> hunger
> loneliness
> struggle
> futility
> despair
> time
> waiting
> fear
> panic
> survival
> duration
> fantasy
> seven days

time enough to make a world
lose a mind
she held

The statement is suspended above a cleft:
why was her wait so long?

In 1921 the Assiniboine region was wild. From Magog, Gog, by Wonder Pass to Marvel Lake, by Gloria and Terrapin to Marvel Pass and Eon's base there was no trail.

A photo taken the year before by Dr. Stone reveals the

panoramic sweep of Mounts Gloria, Eon, Aye, a picture lingered over for a year in Lafayette, placed in the mosaic by Mrs. Stone.

Dr. and Mrs. Stone, "anxious to crown a big one," sought the mystery and the reward, but sought them cautiously. In yielding to the mountain, they found, leaving unanswered, the questions they have become: Dr. Stone, an Icarus, falling from peak, and Margaret Stone a Tantalus in thirst, Prometheus below an eagle-circled sky.

Time burns their personalities away. Pieced photos show the mountain and their route from Marvel Pass.

Why was her agony so long?

The Stones were expected back at the summer climbing camp, the Jubilee Camp of the Alpine Club at Assiniboine, a day after their accident occurred.

The first evening and night that Mrs. Stone spent below the summit, the Stones were supposed to be descending.

Her first full day, when she descended to the ledges, they were to be returning.

Her second day, the entrapment, the people in the camp spent in darkening doubt about their safety.

The third day a party made its way to Marvel Pass and found the Stones' camp. A full reconnaissance was made the fourth day, two days after the Stones were supposed to have returned. Help was sent for in Banff, but Mount Assiniboine is a full day's travel from the town.

The fifth day, Bill Peyto, packer, and Rudolf Aemmer, the Swiss guide, made the forty-five miles to Assiniboine in one day. The sixth day Peyto and Aemmer moved to Marvel Pass.

The seventh day was spent in the search. "It was growing late, when they were startled by hearing a call from a point to the westward."

Help could have come sooner had it come directly from Assiniboine, but no one in the camp believed he had the competence to effect a rescue.

"They discovered Mrs. Stone on a ledge almost a quarter of a mile away and 300 feet below them."

The final photo in the albums is of the summit cairn erected by the men who brought back the body of Winthrop Stone, and noted by her pen's white ink on the black paper.

Part Three

The essentials: earth, air, fire
the mountains strip the rest away and leave
bare rock in wind and sun

The blood of lichens, the green of trees
the mountains leave behind

They move in titans' time
slow
imperceptibly altering from age to age
apart from life
void of life
a taunt of time

The epilogue tells less

In late September, 1975, I wrote Purdue
where Winthrop Stone was President
inquiring if it were known
what had become of Mrs. Stone
learned she had moved from Lafayette in 1923
or so
It was not known where she had gone

The legend of the ledge persists

In late November, '75 on an off chance
I mentioned the mystery to Evelyn Moorhouse

who asked
if the Stones were members of the Alpine Club

Rotting layer cakes
they look like Parthenons or Roman temples
and fall apart by a hand's tug or a stiff wind

Club records indicate in 1923 that Mrs. Stone
life member
moved to Sheffield in the Berkshires
there lived till 1967 or thereabouts

the records for that year say "address unknown"
and then her name disappears from the rolls

Lakes below glimmer, gathering indigo

I wrote the town clerk, Sheffield, heard no more

Too close, you sidle too near

In May of '76, a day low hung with clouds
and snow upon the summits of the rounded mountains
where Melville first met Hawthorne
by Stockbridge where Norman Rockwell lives
Walt Kelly lived
and Alice's Restaurant closed down that month
where Daniel Chester French had his studio
south of Tanglewood and Lenox
by Great Barrington and Sheffield Plain

we proceeded to Sheffield
a small, secluded Berkshires town

Minnie Markham, town clerk, born in Sheffield, 1926
had never heard of Mrs. Stone

Enthralled by the story

The legend of the ledge persists

Warren Wesley, postmaster of Sheffield since the war
had never heard of Mrs. Stone

The legend of the ledge persists

Wisps of cloud move about the mountain's slopes

Storms pass, the mountain wears away
Ice forms on the summit about the cairn topped by his axe
erected to his memory

The ledge is silent

Unseen since and still
the ledge is silent

July 27, 1976
September 8, 1976
March 10, 1977

The Spell of the Yukon
Robert W. Service

I wanted the gold, and I sought it;
   I scrabbled and mucked like a slave.
Was it famine or scurvy — I fought it;
   I hurled my youth into a grave.
I wanted the gold, and I got it —
   Came out with a fortune last fall, —
Yet somehow life's not what I thought it,
   And somehow the gold isn't all.

I've stood in some mighty-mouthed hollow
   That's plumb-full of hush to the brim;
I've watched the big, husky sun wallow
   In crimson and gold, and grow dim,
Till the moon set the pearly peaks gleaming,
   And the stars tumbled out, neck and crop;
And I've thought that I surely was dreaming,
   With the peace o' the world piled on top.

The winter! the brightness that blinds you,
   The white land locked tight as a drum,
The cold fear that follows and finds you,
   The silence that bludgeons you dumb.
The snows that are older than history,

The woods where the weird shadows slant;
The stillness, the moonlight, the mystery,
   I've bade 'em good-by — but I can't.

There's a land where the mountains are nameless,
   And the rivers all run God knows where;
There are lives that are erring and aimless,
   And deaths that just hang by a hair;
There are hardships that nobody reckons;
   There are valleys unpeopled and still;
There's a land — oh, it beckons and beckons,
   And I want to go back — and I will.

The Bootlegger
A. L. Freebairn

In days gone by, when the West was dry,
   Back in eighteen seventy-nine,
Old Nosey Ford brought in a load
   Of 'red-eye' from the line.
He knew right well he'd sure get hell
   If the Mounted Force got wise
So a short way back from his old log shack
   He cached his merchandise.

Then it seemed each day, in a casual way,
   He'd wander down to bring
With an old tin can, just like any man,
   Some water from the spring.
But the thirsty knew, and they were not few,
   Where liquor could be got,
And the old 'blind pig' was going big
   At fifty cents a shot.

Till Sergeant Brail of the town detail,
    A suspicious sort of guy,
Says, "I'll bet my stripes there's booze by cripes,
    In Nosey's — or close by."
So plans were made for a whiskey raid
    On the shack at the end of town.
Brail, with some more, knocked on the door,
    With a warrant from the Crown.

"Come in, come in, and stop your din,"
    Was Nosey's kind invite;
"Just playin' cards with two, three pards
    That happened in tonight.
They'll all agree suspectin' me
    Is all a lot of bosh;
But search you may, and by the way,
    I'll give my hands a wash."

He dumped the can into a pan
    And gave himself a wash,
He lathered well, and sure as hell
    That man had nerve by gosh.
He threw the suds out in the mud
    Liquor, of course, but could the Force
Still prove it any more.

So ends the tale of the bootleg trail
    That led from Whiskey Gap
To Fort Macleod and the old time crowd,
    That put it on the map;
For Nosey Ford, with his next big load,
    Was caught by Sergeant Brail,
And you bet, by gosh, 'ere he could wash
    Was safely locked in jail.

The Last Great Train Robbery

Ted Ferguson

The Old West was gone. Model A Fords rumbled along 35 miles of paved streets in Edmonton, the Calgary telephone lines buzzed with news of massive oil finds, and people in both cities were crowding into moviehouses to watch Mack Sennett comedies. Tom Basoff, a stocky, weather-leathered ranch hand, tried to remain unaffected by the dramatic social changes. He still wore a Stetson and a cowhide vest, rode a horse everywhere, and kept an 1890's model Smith-Wesson in his bedroom dresser.

On August 2, 1920, Basoff took the gun from the drawer and rode to the CPR station in Lethbridge; he had resolved to relive the era of the western outlaws he admired as a youth. He was going to commit the Canadian West's great train robbery.

Basoff had two accomplices, Alex Auloff and George Akoff. All three were of Russian peasant stock. Their parents had migrated to Canada and endured the crushing poverty of a homesteader's life in Alberta. When he was 14, Basoff quit school to work on a string of sheep farms and cattle ranches. What extra money he could squeeze from his meagre wages he used to buy magazines and books about such legendary villains as Butch Cassidy, Black Bart and Jesse James. He was enthralled by the idea of downtrodden cowboys improving their lot through daring acts of banditry.

Auloff and Akoff didn't share his interest in outlaws and the vanished West: they simply wanted to get enough money to form a partnership and purchase a ranch.

The decision to rob CPR train No. 63 on its run from Lethbridge to Cranbrook B.C., came after Basoff learned in a casual conversation that the so-called King of the Bootleggers, Emilio Picariello, planned to be aboard. Operating out of Blairmore, Alta. Picariello amassed a fortune during

Prohibition smuggling booze across the Canada-U.S. border in a fleet of Model T cars. He was a big spender and was known to carry rolls of money in his pockets. By robbing Picariello and the other 30-odd passengers, the trio figured they would have a sizeable haul — and with much less risk than if they assaulted a well-guarded bank.

There had not been a train hold-up in the province for at least 20 years. The advent of the telephone, faster trains, stronger express cars and police units using automobiles had convinced railroad officials that such capers belonged to the past.

Conductor Sam Jones discovered otherwise at 5 p.m. on that warm autumn day. The train was just outside Coleman, Alta., when the slightly-built CPR veteran heard strange voices in a men's lavatory and opened the door to investigate. Basoff immediately jammed his Smith-Wesson in the conductor's stomach.

"You must be drinking," Jones said. "Put the gun away. It could go off."

"It will if you don't do what you're told," Basoff replied.

The second man in the small compartment, Auloff, drew a Mauser automatic and the two thieves forced Jones to walk to the crowded first-class coach. Akoff was already there and, upon seeing his companions, he too pulled out a pistol.

The shocked passengers watched in disbelief as the trio produced an empty suitcase and instructed everyone to place their money and valuables inside it. To the bandits' chagrin, the man they thought was Picariello turned out to be an unemployed labourer: the bootlegger had missed the train.

Jones was left near the back of the wicker-seated car, sitting next to a young man. "Why don't you pull the signal cord," the passenger whispered to him. "They're too busy to notice."

Jones complied. Reaching above his head, he yanked the cord once, triggering a whistle in the locomotive cab. Basoff turned in time to see him do it and fired a shot. The bullet burrowed into the woodwork half an inch from Jones' hand and the conductor dropped back down on his seat.

In the train's signal system, one pull on the cord meant stop at the next station to let passengers off; two pulls meant halt the train immediately. Engineer George Alexander, having not the slightest inkling that anything was amiss, took Jones' single pull to mean that the train should stop at the next village, Sentinel.

Basoff and his accomplices searched the men to make sure they'd donated all their costly possessions. They didn't search the women and several men passed their wallets to their wives who hid them under their dresses. Two businessmen kept their cash by stuffing it in their socks and a third male shoved $1,000 in bills under a seat cushion. At one point Basoff tossed 65 cents back to a man saying, "Keep it for your supper. You look like you need a meal."

When they finished with the passengers, two of the thieves went into other cars to rob the crew. They took $25 from baggageman J. H. Staples and $40 from brakeman Walter Hickey. Then Auloff made a move that was to prove his undoing eventually — he snatched Jones' pocket watch, breaking the gold chain to get it. The watch was an easily-recognizable gold Elgin that the conductor had bought two weeks earlier for $96 (roughly a month's wages).

While Auloff was keeping an eye on the passengers, Basoff and Akoff were in the express car, listening to a frightened clerk insist that he did not have the combination for the safe. Suddenly, the train stopped.

The two men hurried back to the first-class coach.

"What's going on?" Basoff asked Jones.

"A routine stop," the conductor said. "We're at Sentinel."

The robbers didn't believe him. They jumped off the train and Basoff yelled at the surprised engineer, telling him to take the train on to Cranbrook. To ensure its rapid exit, he fired a shot over the engineer's head. No. 63 started up and, gaining speed, barrelled five miles to the next station where Jones alighted and telegraphed the authorities.

The robbery caused a sensation. Newspapers across the country carried front-page stories about the burly fellows with Russian accents. Many quoted Freda Bundy, the wife of a CPR agent who blurted out, "But people simply don't go around robbing trains anymore!"

The bandits' booty was small — roughly $300 in bills and valuables — yet the authorities treated the crime as though it were a million dollar heist. They assigned their best men to the case for if the trio escaped punishment, their action could spur a rash of similar robberies.

RCMP, Alberta Provincial police and the railway police all sought the thieves. So did a small army of armed civilians and a half dozen Indian trackers from the East Kootenay region. But despite the blanket coverage, the three men avoided detection. Basoff and Akoff went south and rented rooms in a Bellevue brothel: Auloff crossed the border into Montana and headed for the West Coast.

Five days after the hold-up, Basoff and his friend went for a walk along the main street of the coal-mining community. Stopping in front of Justice of the Peace Joseph Robertson's office, they shared a laugh as they read a Wanted poster on an outside bulletin board. Their descriptions were accurate — even down to the fact that the ringleader had a glass eye — but the pair felt that the last place the police would ever look would be a brothel less than 30 miles from the scene of the crime.

Robertson, however, happened to pass them on the sidewalk and glancing at Basoff, recognized him by the glass eye. He watched them enter a Chinese cafe and then he ran to the local APP office. The three lawmen inside — RCMP Corporal Ernest Usher and APP constables Jimmy Frewin and Fred Bailey — listened intently when he told them where to find the duo.

Frewin went into the cafe first, a gun in each pocket of his tweed jacket. Basoff and Akoff were in a booth near the back of the near-empty cafe. At a pre-arranged signal Usher came through the front door and Bailey the rear. All three lawmen drew their guns.

"You're under arrest," Frewin said, approaching the booth. "Put your hands in the air."

Akoff reached under the table and brought up a Luger. Frewin fired, mortally wounding him. As Akoff slumped forward Basoff leapt from the booth and collided with Usher. The Mountie's gun went off, hitting the bandit in the leg. More shots rang out and Basoff, the cowboy who dreamed of being a romantic outlaw, was now a murderer. His Smith-Wesson barked five times, killing Bailey and Usher and badly wounding Frewin. Akoff rose and, bleeding profusely, managed to get to the street, where he collapsed and died. Basoff limped from the cafe and fled. Robertson, crouching behind a telephone pole, emptied a .22 pistol at Basoff's back but missed on every shot.

The death of the two lawmen brought more than 200 armed civilians and police into southern Alberta. The RCMP issued a warning for searchers not to turn the affair into a lynch party. The night after the cafe shooting a civilian searcher was shot and killed when a policeman, seeing him climb from a shack window carrying a gun, gathered he was Basoff.

Basoff continued to elude his pursuers. For three days and nights, lawmen and civilians scoured practically every mining shack, every vehicle, every farmhouse in the Bellevue region. Three bloodhounds were driven in from Seattle, Washington. But they too failed. Taken to the cafe and given Basoff's cap to sniff, the $5,000 hounds sprinted in three different directions!

Then the searchers got a break. CPR engineer Harold Hammond was peering into the black night from the cab of his speeding locomotive when a stocky man suddenly limped across the tracks a few miles outside of Pincher. Even in the fleeting locomotive light Hammond realized the man must be Basoff.

He picked up four CPR constables further along the line and took them back to Pincher. Leaving the train, the heavily-armed quartet walked into town and around 11 p.m. spotted the wanted man sitting near a stockyard shed, disguised as a hobo. He was eating a tin of bullybeef and a bag of cookies he'd bought from a local merchant earlier. The foursome swooped down, guns drawn, before he had a chance to move.

Basoff was eventually convicted of Bailey's murder and hanged.

That left Auloff still at large.

APP Assistant-Superintendent J. D. Nicholson directed the manhunt. A former RCMP officer, Nicholson was renowned for his diligent detective work and especially the gathering of evidence that led to the conviction of a notorious Edmonton murderer, William Oscar King.

In 1906 King robbed and killed farmer Joseph Hindahl but, lacking solid evidence, the police could not charge him. Nicholson tracked down clues throughout Alberta and the northern United States linking King to the death. Ironically, one of these clues was a watch King took from the victim — an Elgin similar to the one that was to seal Auloff's fate.

Nicholson picked up Auloff's trail at the border and followed it to the northwestern United States. Several times he came close to catching the robber who was working at odd jobs in lumber camps and small towns in Washington and Oregon. But Auloff stayed one jump ahead. He seemed to have many friends who warned him whenever Nicholson turned up asking questions.

Reluctantly Nicholson returned home to attack a mounting pile of paperwork. In his place he assigned detective Ernest Schoeppe. Auloff was sticking close to the Russian communities and as Schoeppe spoke Russian Nicholson reasoned that he had a better chance of apprehending him.

For three months, the sturdy, six foot detective wandered

around the West Coast, pretending he was a laborer and an old friend of Auloff's from Alberta. He, too, barely missed the holdup man several times and again warned that someone was asking about him, Auloff decided to leave the country for a while. He went south and vanished into Mexico. Learning he was gone, Schoeppe went back to Alberta.

On January 18, 1924, a detective in Portland, Oregon, sent Schoeppe a telegram. A watch identical to the one Auloff took from the conductor Jones had been found in a local pawnshop. Schoeppe hurried to Portland, picked up the watch and traced its ownership to an unemployed miner, Ali Hassen.

"I'm no train robber," Hassen declared. "I got the watch from a guy I worked with in Butte, Montana. He lost it in a poker game."

"What did he look like?" Schoeppe inquired.

"A heavy-set fellow. He had a bit of an accent. Russian, I think."

Schoeppe was off to Butte that very day. It took him six hours of making inquiries in the Montana town to find a boarding house owner who said Auloff, using an alias, was living there. When the train robber came home after his shift at a mine, Schoeppe arrested him.

"You've got the wrong man," Auloff said. "I'm from Alberta but I don't know any Basoff or Akoff."

On the train north, Schoeppe deliberately pulled out Jones' watch and held it up in front of Auloff's face. The robber broke down and confessed to the crime. "That bloody watch," he grumbled. "Why didn't I throw it away?"

The watch was used as evidence at the trial which resulted in a seven-year sentence for Auloff. When the trial ended, conductor Jones retrieved the gold Elgin and he looked at it every day for the remainder of his railroad career.

Harvester Patrol

T. Morris Longstreth

An entire car in the eastbound Canadian Pacific flier had been reserved for the Mounted Police. It was August. The crop was going to be huge, possibly a record-breaker. There were not enough idle men in the whole West to harvest it. The East was being called upon, and on both railways great excursions with as many as 1,200 men to a train would soon be rolling westward. The Mounted Police, two or three men to a train, were to accompany them as guards, advisors, and chaperons, for a thousand men off on such a holiday are not always wise or gentle.

Constable Bourlois had a double interest in the trip, for he had not finished his course at Regina, and this would not only be his first patrol, it would be his first visit home since he had donned the uniform. Bourlois was sitting with three other men of greater experience, listening to an argument as to the most important date in the Force's history.

"What about 1873?" Constable Henry was insisting. "If the outfit hadn't got going, there would have been no dates to follow, hence '73 is the source of all important dates, therefore, the most important."

"You're full of hay," said Corporal Tanner. "1920's the date. Then we finally came into our own."

"Now you're starting to talk," said Alton, an older constable, "but you can't name the most important date because it hasn't arrived. The day that the Dominion wakes up to the fact that the whole country can be more effectively and economically policed by one force instead of by half a dozen, that day's going to be our big date."

"It's coming," said Tanner.

"Of course it's coming," retorted Alton, "and sooner than anyone thinks."

"How soon?" asked Bourlois.

"The day when the last province asks us to do for it what we're doing for Saskatchewan and Alberta and the Territories now."

Bourlois' eyes shone as they forecast the time ahead. Already the work was infinitely varied. In 1920, fourteen thousand new cases demanded attention by the Police, and fourteen thousand is a large number. Men were often working months on a single case, seeing that money was not being counterfeited, preventing drugs from being smuggled into the country, stopping illegal lobster-potting, keeping immigrants from sneaking in, protecting bird sanctuaries from violation, looking after the betting at race tracks, smoothing down obstreperous Indians on the Eastern reserves. It seemed as if new services were demanded by one or another department of the Government every day. Even this harvester patrol was new, and it came at the most inconvenient time of the year. But there was one great advantage of being busy; it proved that the Force was a necessity. Bourlois, who was an ambitious, dark-eyed French Canadian with a perfect command of both tongues, hoped that the awakening of politicians would soon come.

Bourlois lived in Hull, opposite Ottawa, and his visit home was a little triumph. His family admired the uniform, exclaimed over how he had expanded into it, and wondered at his knowledge, the slang from barracks, at least the little that it was prudent to air. His twenty hours' leave seemed but twenty minutes, but he had orders to present himself at "N" Division at six o'clock, where he was paraded before the officer commanding for instruction. He found that Corporal Tanner and he were to have charge of one train.

"Your object," said the inspector, "is to maintain law and order en route to Winnipeg. Much damage has been done on unescorted trains in previous years. Your duty is to prevent it. The situations that arise will require tact and firmness. This duty will be new to the harvesters, as well as to yourselves, and they will be tempted to try their old tricks. Much depends on your treatment of the first situation. Let nothing get out of hand. It will be advisable for you to search the train for weapons and liquor. I must emphasize the need for constant watchfulness. Your train, Corporal, pulls out at 12:05 tonight. Constable Bourlois will report to you at Union Station not later than 10:30."

As the evening wore along, Bourlois felt a nervous tension creeping over him. He found the Corporal, and wondered whether Tanner really felt as cool as he looked. Now that he was face to face with the collecting harvesters, the job seemed one to breed emergencies. Tanner was about thirty, a blond Westerner with wide blue eyes, a brief moustache, and big shoulders. He had seen six years' service.

"Ever do anything like this before?" asked Bourlois, trying to appear nonchalant.

"Never had the chance. I've been rusticating at Simpson the last three years. There are more people waiting for this train than lived between us and the Pole. A swell lot of harvesters they'll make. Look at them."

Bourlois' glance wandered from group to group in the congested waiting-room. Hard seeds, many of them, floaters who were intending to earn enough on the harvest field to put them through the winter. He noticed young fellows who might be bank clerks or grocers' assistants, with whitish faces. Some fellow French Canadians, dark-faced from the summer fields, bore their food with them. Four chaps who had obviously made merry on strong drink were playing cards on a suitcase table. Bourlois spotted them as likely trouble-makers. He wished that the gates would open, that the ordeal would begin; the waiting brought an inner uneasiness.

The train, he was amazed to find, was nineteen cars long, with tourist coach accommodation for the men. He stood near Tanner at the gate as the stream of harvesters pushed through. Their scarlet was a surprise to the crowd.

"Didn't I tell you?" asked one fellow in a beery good

humour, "we're goin' to 'ave an hescort, just like the Gov'nor Jin'ral."

The brakeman spoke to Tanner with a clear sense of relief. "Glad to have you running the show this year boys. The railway couldn't stand another year like last. It sure was a corker. It's a wonder more wasn't killed, the ructions them rowdies raised."

"Killed?" echoed Bourlois, surprised.

The brakeman rolled an eye at him. "There's a lot happened last year the papers didn't print."

"Well, they won't have much to print this year, either," said Tanner, "but for a different reason. Come on, Bourlois, we'd better find a place to bunk."

"Look in the tenth car," advised the brakeman. "The conductor's put a couple of mattresses in the smoking compartment. It'll be handy for you."

By the time the two had disposed their kits in the compartment, the train was pulling out.

"Where do we go from here?" asked Bourlois.

"We'll start in and search the train for liquor. I'll begin at the rear, you up front. Ask about firearms, too."

Bourlois wanted to say "And what if there's trouble?" but his pride forbade, and he set out for the engine full of energy and apprehension. The train was endless. Through lurching car after lurching car he walked, simulating a dignity he did not feel. His charges were already at home, smoking, hauling themselves upon their shelves in stocking feet, playing cards. They paid little attention to him, and this helped.

To his surprise the front coach was full of women. Then he remembered that the harvesters required cooks on the great farms, and these women were going out to help over the stove.

"No firearms or flasks, ladies?" he called out jocularly from the door. A laugh greeted this.

"Come and see, Mounty," they dared him. He had made friends with the carful. The good-looking youth in the handsome uniform wished that all the harvesters were women.

After telling them to send for him if anyone tried to be fresh, he closed the door, sure of allies.

Nor was the beginning of his search any harder. He moved quietly from seat to seat asking the men the same question, looking into battered suitcases, feeling mackinaw pockets, judging from the face he interrogated as to whether a search was required. In the sixth car, however, trouble raised its head. He had collected a small arm-load of bottles, and stopped before the card-players he had noticed in the station.

"Suppose you give me that bottle," he said quietly.

"What bottle?" demanded one player loudly.

"The bottle between your legs. Hand it over, please."

"Come and take it," he retorted sullenly.

It is only training that makes instantaneous reactions skilful. Bourlois did not reason out that to reach for the bottle, to have to scuffle for it, especially with several under his arm, would diminish the prestige of his standing. Instinct told him to go to the root of the matter. With an arm and a wrist made strong by much handling of unruly horseflesh, he reached for the man's collar and brought him to his feet, had him out on the aisle, stood him there. "I asked you civilly for that bottle," said the constable. "Now you keep out of the way while I take it."

The other, surprised at the suddenness of the constable's attack, and impressed by its force, stood there while Bourlois picked up the bottle, none of the rest interfering. "We've a long ride together," said Bourlois, "I want it to be pleasant. So do you, don't you?"

They agreed, Bourlois went on, feeling better. His first encounter had been successful.

But he had not reached home yet. His ears were assailed in the next car by a laboured but stentorian singing. Some of the men were trying to stop the music for sleep's sake. They hailed Bourlois. "Hey Mounty, shove this fellow off the train." "Make him shut up, Mounty."

The fellow, as Bourlois saw at once, had drowned his

common sense in beer, and was unmistakably ugly. At the same moment, the chap's drunken attention was caught by the uniform, also by the bottles in the constable's arms.

"Where are you going with that beer, brother? Give me a drink," and he made a lurch at the load.

Bourlois dodged the man's grasp. "Is that your berth?" he asked.

"Sure it's my berth, and what of it? You can't drink all that, brother."

"Get your shoes off and go to bed. You need to sleep it off."

"Who're you ordering me around? I ain't going to bed. I'm going to give these fellows a song. Want to hear a song, pal?"

Bourlois was conscious of the crowd in the aisles, pressing closer, and now a laugh came from them.

"It's too late for singing," said Bourlois. "Close up for the night. Get your shoes off. I'm waiting till you do."

At that the man burst into a roar of melody. Bourlois put the bottles down. "Cut that racket," he ordered. "Stop it."

Instantly the man turned ugly. "Come and stop it. See that?" and he drew a knife from a sheath. "That'll stop you, if you don't shut up and go away."

Light glinted from the sharp blade. The man had taken a step forward, raising his knife. Men called Bourlois to come back. But he knew what he was about. The train lurched around a curve. Picking up a harvester's bundle of clothing, Bourlois fired it in the man's face. The combination was too much for the unsteady one's legs. As he swayed, blinded, the constable took the arm in a firm grip and wrenched the knife from its hold.

"Now will you climb out of your clothes and go to sleep?" demanded Bourlois, "or shall I use these?" and he dangled a pair of handcuffs before the man's eyes.

The singer was sufficiently sobered to see the advantages of freedom, and Bourlois pursued his way. This incident closed the adventures for the night. Bourlois found that Tanner had collected several weapons and considerable booze. It was four of the morning and the landscape was starting to grey.

"Where do we eat?" asked the constable.

"At wayside restaurants. Our job's to see that the poor hunky-dories aren't charged three prices. That was the chief reason for the riots last summer. The cafes thought they had a cinch."

Fortunately, breakfast required neither tact nor firmness, as the train halted by a railway restaurant. Also, many of the men had brought rations for the first part of the trip. By noon Bourlois felt that he had lived on the train a week. The heat, the dust through a hundred windows, the lack of sleep, were sufficiently wearing. But the need of alertness was doubly exacting. He had to look spruce, keep watchful, and seem outwardly unofficial, as sense told him that an air of friendliness which never became familiarity was best.

Already cliques were forming in the different cars. The French Canadians gravitated to each other. Shanty-men found other shanty-men to talk to. The young bloods on adventure bent found a dozen ways of being hilarious. One of these, a scrawny indefatigable teaser, delighted in plaguing the man who, the night before, had sought to sing the car awake. Arguments throve, rose to the edge of blows, and then — the scarlet-coated guardian would be seen, and the blows were not delivered. That was the strain of it for Tanner and Bourlois, always managing to be casually on hand where disturbance might be brewing.

In that crowd, events came to a head quickly. One man played distressingly on the mouth-organ. A young French Canadian, quick and tempermental, threatened his teeth for it. The organist wheezed on. With a grab and a pitch the mouth-organ flew out the window. The owner was a large man with a close-shaven bulletish head. With an oath he charged the pea-souper and, lifting him bodily, began to stuff him out of the window of the moving train. The French Canadian, clinging desperately, yelled for help. His fellows were soon at the man's rump, beating a tattoo on it. A first-class row was in the making when Corporal Tanner appeared.

Tanner was strong. In an instant he had got to the organist and dragged him into the aisle. The French Canadian wriggled to safety. Voices clouded the air. Tanner waited for a lull and then said, "This train stops in ten minutes. Both of you men will leave it unless I have a promise."

"Spit it out," growled the organ-player.

"You'll keep your hands off this boy till we reach Winnipeg."

"But he t'rew my mout-organ out of de window."

"And you," said Tanner to the French Canadian, "will buy this man a mouth-organ when you reach Winnipeg."

"I will like hell."

"Suit yourself," said Tanner, "you know the alternative. It will cost you considerably more."

Before the next stop was reached the young man had given his word.

It was by small but important decisions like this that the peace was kept. The main body of the crowd was by nature orderly and submissive. One old habitant from Quebec had brought his fiddle, and never lacked an audience. There were bright young fellows who had tasted of half a dozen businesses and were out to sample another. Bourlois, strolling up and down the train, soon picked out men with whom he had pleasure in exchanging a word, and others whom he wished he could avoid. And presently the first twenty-four hours rolled around. Neither Mounted Policeman had closed an eye.

"We'll try watches, tonight," said Tanner. "You hit the hay at midnight and I'll wake you at three. I'll turn in till six. How's that sound?"

"Suits me," said Bourlois, but he was almost too tired to sleep in their oven of a compartment and he had only dropped off, it seemed, when he felt a hand on his shoulder. "Six o'clock, fellow."

"Six?" The light showed that it was so. "But you . . . you were to wake me at three," said Bourlois, sleepily realizing Tanner's considerate act.

Tanner laughed. "I was enjoying myself. Met a chap from Australia. He's taking this train for economy. Quite a globetrotter. Maybe I'll sleep this morning."

Bourlois knew that he wouldn't, but sacrifice like this was common, it was what pulled the men in the outfit together, and the constable resolved that he would make it up to Tanner in some way.

The second day was worse than the first, hotter, dirtier. The 1,100 passengers were showing the strain of uncomfortable inaction, their tempers were fraying. Thunder was in the air, and a sullen atmosphere distinguished one of the cars particularly. Bourlois felt conscious of the change in attitude. Sullen looks, sly looks, whispers. Something was being plotted.

"I'm turning in for an hour," said the corporal, "if you can manage."

"Go ahead," said Bourlois. The boy wanted to mention the feeling that all was not right in car 17, but disliked seeming to keep Tanner up.

"Wake me if you need me," urged the corporal.

"I won't need you. They're eating out of my hand," replied Bourlois, with an air of assurance that surprised even himself. But he kept a sharper eye, was quicker to stop altercations, and ardently wished that the train did not have to stop. The waits were worst of all. It was then that the men mingled on the platform and displayed their bravado, their tricks. At one siding, several of them had started a brush fire for the deviltry of it; luckily the Policeman had seen it at the outset and had it stopped.

About half an hour after Tanner had gone to sleep, the worst combination occurred: the long harvester special had to pull out on a siding to let one of the great expresses through, and Bourlois learned from the brakeman that the express was twenty-five minutes late. Should he call Tanner? No, he decided, not until needed, anyway. Bourlois had pride, and also he felt grateful for his unbroken sleep. So, looking his neatest and most regimental, he started to patrol the platform. Groups of weary harvesters stood idly about. Bourlois noticed one party of seven or eight young men disappearing up the street of the town in a hurry. From more than one overheard remark the constable gathered that some mischief was being planned.

"Where are those chaps going, do you know?" he asked.

"Don't ask me, buddy," came the too familiar reply.

Instantly the constable's apprehensions took form. He caught sight of two of the toughest looking over their shoulders at the place where the party had vanished. "Sshh!" he overheard, "here comes the Mounty."

Obviously something unpleasant was afoot. He must think quickly. He could not follow the party, leaving a thousand men to their own devices. Yet he must put a stop to any trick that these restless youths might try to play upon the townspeople.

A harvester sauntered up, and Bourlois recognized a man who had cut himself and whom he had mended with his first aid kit. This harvester sidled close with a studiously casual air and said, "Look out for trouble. A bunch of guys is out to get even on this place for last year."

"How so?"

"Last year they was beat up by a storekeeper here, their own fault, too, for trying to raid him. Now they're going to beat him up."

"How far's the store?"

"About three blocks in." The harvester started to move away. "You needn't let on I said anything."

"Thanks, I won't," said Bourlois. He knew what he would do, and he would not have to wake Tanner. The constable walked rapidly to the engineer. "Ring the bell, will you please. I'm trying to stop some monkey-business. I want them to think you're leaving."

The engineer looked at his watch. "I can do better than that for you. I'll pull up the line for a minute or two. The other train's not in for eighteen minutes."

"Thanks."

At once the whistle blew, the bell rang, all the strollers and loafers on the platform jumped aboard. The train began to puff black smoke, to inch along. Bourlois walked back to the rear car, swung aboard himself. They had not moved two hundred yards up the track before he saw the first of the raiding party, then the others, racing towards the train. The engineer must have seen them, too, for he pushed the throttle ahead. The train was gaining on them, going faster than a man could run. The gang came hot-footing it down the ties. The leader tripped and sprawled. Two others fell over him. They picked themselves up. By this time the back-platform was crowded by a company of harvesters, hooting, jeering, laughing; for it required little to shift the allegiance of this company

When Bourlois was satisfied, he pulled the cord, the train stopped. The raiders straggled aboard, blown and hot and sheepish. With notebook in hand, the constable got their names. "You men are lucky," he said, "you've probably just escaped arrest." Bourlois pulled the cord again. The train began to push back upon the siding. The crowd, comprehending the trick, bellowed with laughter.

"What did you do to them, Riarty?" called a harvester.

"Nothin', we hadn't hardly reached the store when this — bell rang."

"You're lucky, as the Mounty says," shouted another. "You can't fool this here red-coat."

Bourlois' victory was complete. A moment later he saw Tanner's serge approaching. But the trouble was over. It was over for the trip. Bourlois' good-nature, together with his firmness and swift thinking, had held up his end. Twenty-four hours later the party disembarked at Winnipeg, and good wishes were exchanged between Mounted Policemen and their charges at the gates. The two sought barracks, to report. Both were very tired, but the patrol had been successfully concluded; that would stand, that fact, while the tiredness could be cured.

Constable Bourlois was surprised at the nonchalance with which they were received. A nod, a single question, "Good trip?" and then the surface of current affairs closed over them again. Could it be, Bourlois wondered, that such an epoch-making display of firmness and tact should be accepted as a matter of course? Apparently it was. He glanced at Tanner, who had sat down at a desk to write out his report. The corporal did not seem disturbed by any lack of hurrah. Bourlois decided that he had learned one more thing about the Force: you were expected to succeed.

Tanner beckoned him over, held up a page for him to see. Bourlois read: "I may say in closing that Constable Bourlois handled several delicate situations with tact and firmness. His conduct of affairs at all times was more than satisfactory."

"That's good of you," Bourlois flushed at this official commendation.

"We're always supposed to understate in reports," smiled Tanner. "That's the official way of saying you did damned well."

"It wasn't so hard, with you along," said Bourlois.

The sergeant major stepped up. "Seen orders yet, men? You two are to hop back to Montreal and bring out another harvester special."

The Barber of Barkerville
Cecil Clark

On a sultry afternoon in early August 1866, Wellington Delaney Moses, boom town Barkerville's Negro barber, beckoned his next customer to the establishment's single chair. Next customer, as it happened, was one of the town gamblers, a tall, hard-faced Texan called James Barry who slung his broad-brimmed felt hat on a nearby peg and with a curt nod of half recognition to Moses took his seat. The two had met before on brief occasions, but Barry the southerner, held fast to his ingrained ideas about colour.

As Moses leaned over Barry's shoulder, slipping the white sheet under his customer's chin, he suddenly paused. As he looked down he eyed something on the gambler's black string tie. It was a gold nugget stick pin that suddenly held the barber's attention. Although it was only a split second pause yet it started a chain of events that 12 months later ended with Barry's sudden death. At the end of a rope!

After Barry there were other customers, mostly miners, of the shaggy variety who, after "clean up" of a week or two's backbreaking rock work were now in the process of cleaning up for an evening of Barkerville night life.

It was late that night when Moses finally closed up and retired to his bedroom behind the barber shop. Thoughts of Barry's nugget pin returned to him now and again. It sort of worried him, because in a vague way he felt he'd seen it before. But where he couldn't recall. On this night, like many others, Moses found it hard to get to sleep, mainly because on the other side of the pitch pine wall was Ross and Burdick's dance hall and saloon. Long after midnight, through the rough siding, the hoot and stamp of miners and girls was backgrounded by the frenzied sawing of fiddlers. It was as the barber lay awake in the dark there came a sudden flash of recognition. The nugget pin belonged to Blessing! He was sure of it. There couldn't be another like it.

To gauge the proper significance of "Del" Moses discovery requires a little history, history which started eight years back in Victoria when the summer of 1858 saw the miners pouring in from California.

Wellington Delaney Moses was one of the throng that first pitched tents, then hastily threw up wooden buildings with whipsawed lumber, and ended up building with bricks, mortar and stone.

Despite the fact that water was a scarce commodity (a man peddled it from a horse-drawn barrel at 40 buckets for a dollar) there were still those who wanted a shave and a haircut. On July 29, 1858, Del Moses opened Victoria's first barber shop, which offered the additional luxury of a bath.

The Cariboo mining boom of the middle 1860's that made Barkerville the biggest town in the Canadian west, pulled Moses in that direction and he opened a barber shop at Williams Creek. Custom was to winter in the south, at either New Westminster or Victoria and barber Moses followed the season trend.

It was in the spring of 1866 when Del Moses was returning to his one-chair shop at Barkerville that passing through Yale he met a man called Charles Morgan Blessing. When they discovered they were both heading in the same direction, they decided to travel together. "Chummies" in the language of the day.

Blessing, 33, stemmed from a wealthy Boston family and had followed the wanderlust for gold, first in California, then in British Columbia. Despite rubbing shoulders in the roughest of mining camps, somehow Blessing had still retained his quiet, well mannered outlook. With no colour consciousness, he apparently found in Moses, the English-born Negro, an independence of mind that few New Englanders had encountered.

Perhaps for this reason the two got along well, travelling

up-river by steamer to Yale, then rattling along the Cariboo road on one of Barnard's six-horse stages, up through the sage brush country to Soda Creek. There they caught the sternwheeler for the 60-mile trip to Quesnel, which they reached about seven o'clock on the evening of May 28. After sizing up shanty town Quesnel, perched on a bench above the river, they turned in, which, in the custom of the country, meant rolling up in their blankets on the floor of Brown and Gillis' saloon, in the mixed company of other tired travellers. At the end of the room the bar kept open, the sleepers oblivious to the noise. If it was rough, it was the mode that every Cariboo traveller followed, whether he was bank manager, miner, policeman, or chief justice.

It was the next afternoon Moses and his friend fell in with James Barry, or rather Barry seemed to slip into their company. Slick and debonair, it was plain to them that if Barry toiled with his hands it wasn't in a mine. To their questions he conceded he had a natural bent for the intricacies of any card game involving money. Blessing suggested they adjourn for a drink and it was then that gambler Barry hesitantly admitted that his card sense had lately gone awry. He was broke.

Blessing opened his wallet at the bar and drew out a $20 Bank of British Columbia note, upon which Moses gave him the quiet tip to avoid spending too much.

Said Blessing with a grin, "I've got a few more of these before I'm broke." Neither apparently noticed the look of sudden interest in Barry's face.

After a few drinks it was agreed that Blessing and Barry would start the next morning for Barkerville, the snakelike 65-mile trail over a hilly route. Moses decided to stay over in Quesnel to hunt up a man who owed him some money. It was that evening, to avoid the crowded sleeping quarters in the saloon, that Barry suggested to Blessing that they bunk down in a nearby vacant shack. With a goodnight to Moses they moved off in the dark. Next morning Moses sought out the shack, but apparently the pair had made an early start. An Indian camped nearby said he'd seen the two men fold their blankets and head for the Barkerville wagon trail about daylight.

The road eastward to Barkerville, blazed by pioneers, was still rough going, beset with mud holes and not only lined with tree stumps but the debris of early day gold seekers, which ranged from tin cans to the whitened bones of horses and mules, mute evidence of the misery and starvation that once marked the path to Eldorado.

When Moses arrived in Barkerville, and looked around for Blessing, he ran into Barry coming out of Jimmy Loring's saloon. The gambler would have passed the barber had not Moses grabbed him by the arm to enquire about his friend.

"Oh, that fellow," drawled Barry, as if he had a hard time recalling him. "He wasn't much good on the trail. Got sore feet or something and quit. I think he went back to Quesnel."

Weeks passed, and as Moses plied his scissors and razor occasionally he thought of his friend Blessing and sometimes asked some newly arrived miner whether he had heard of him. Nobody had.

Barry, meantime, was here and there around Barkerville, Richfield and Camerontown. Though separately named they were all practically one community linked by a mile long, 18-foot wide, main street, distinguished not only for its raucous night life but the size of the chuck holes. The miners had no time for civic improvement. Along this muddy midway the saloons and stores were 50-50. That is, there were 50 of each. Combined with most saloons was a dance hall, with gambling accommodation in the back.

At night, in a bedlam of noise, under the glare of naphtha lamps, each saloon proprietor did his best to separate the miners from their pokes. Added attractions were the "hurdies", big, buxom girls, recruited mainly from Germany and Holland, who invariably wore the distinguishing red blouse, hoop skirts and around their heads a red bandana, the bow on top. Their "day" started about eight in the evening, when for a dollar a dance they were whirled off their feet by exuberant miners to the jigging tempo of fiddle and concertina. After each dance (about one whirl around the floor) the girls led their bearded and booted partners to the bar, where they got a commission on the drinks.

Gambler Barry was at home in this scene and his smooth approach made him a favourite with most of the girls. When he wasn't manipulating cards or dice, he was rated Don Juan of the dance halls.

The missing Blessing had shown Moses his nugget pin on the way up from New Westminster, and when the barber glimpsed it in Barry's tie came the dawning suspicion the gambler might be linked in sinister fashion with Blessing's non-arrival. Moses knew that Blessing thought a lot of the pin and he certainly wouldn't sell it or give it away to a chance acquaintance of Barry's type. Besides, he didn't have to sell it. Blessing had money.

Money? There was a question and a good one. True, Barry was adept at coming out on the right side of a card or dice game, or collecting some of the earnings of some infatuated "hurdy". But how much money did he have when he arrived?

There was something about this that needed looking into, and the next day the methodical Mr. Moses locked his shop and started some discreet enquiries. Finally he got the information he wanted. From Sam Wilcox, boardinghouse keeper, he learned that when Barry first arrived in Barkerville in early June he got a room at Wilcox's at $12 a week. Asked to pay in advance, the man who was broke at Quesnel on May 29 had a $20 Bank of British Columbia bill on June 2. Back in his barbershop bedroom Moses was in two minds whether to tell his story to the British Columbia Police at Richfield. Then he thought better of it. After all it was only suspicion.

A few weeks passed, until on a day in late September Moses

found himself cutting the hair of a miner called Bill Fraser. Fraser had been all up and down the coast since landing in Victoria in '58, and in addition seemed to know a lot of Moses' early-day Victoria customers. Finally Moses asked Fraser if he'd ever run across a gambler called Barry.

"That character!" exclaimed Fraser. "Why? You a friend of his?"

Moses removed any suspicion on this point, but intimated he had an interest in Barry's background. By coincidence Fraser had travelled up from New Westminster with Barry that spring and on the road had figured, from remarks Barry dropped, that the tall Texan had seen the inside of more than one jail. He also seemed to know the inside story of a few recent robberies and when Fraser asked him how he knew, Barry admitted he'd heard about these goings-on from "a fellow who was in the chain gang with me at New Westminster".

On the trip up, went on Fraser, Barry always wore a Colt revolver holstered on his cartridge belt. Fraser was interested in the gun because he had a friend in New Westminster who had just lost one. In fact he had supplied Fraser with the serial number of the missing weapon in case he ran across it. Once or twice on the trip Fraser tried to steer the conversation to guns, thinking to get a chance of examining Barry's weapon. But the gambler never let it out of his possession. "Even slept with it under his pillow," Fraser concluded.

It could have been under his head when he slept alongside Blessing, thought Moses.

Finally, said Fraser, he parted company with his dubious companion at Quesnel. It was the same day that Barry had picked up acquaintance with Moses and Blessing.

The picture was now a little clearer in the barber's mind, so he figured it was time to go to the police.

Next morning in the log-built Richfield police station Moses sought out the ear of Chief Constable W. H. Fitzgerald. The district head of the police listened gravely to the barber's tale.

"A very interesting story, Moses," said Fitzgerald at the conclusion, "and I'll have someone look into it. Meantime if you hear anything more..." It was at that moment he was interrupted by the appearance of Constable John H. Sullivan. "Excuse me Chief," said the Irish born officer (who would one day head the force) "but we've just had word from Bloody Edwards' place. They've found a body there. Looks like murder."

"Any identification?" asked Fitzgerald.

"Yes, a man called Blessing. Charles Morgan Blessing. Ever heard of him?"

In the silence that followed the query Fitzgerald shot a glance at the Barkerville barber. But Moses had suddenly turned to gaze fixedly out of the window.

The immediate police investigation showed that a miner, out shooting grouse near the Edwards' stopping place at Beaver Pass, had been searching just off the road for a wounded bird. Forty feet into the thicket he almost stepped on what he thought was some clothing. But it was clothing that covered all that was left of a man. A jacket pocket yielded a wallet, empty of money, but bearing the name of Charles Morgan Blessing. Nearby was a tin cup with the initials "CMB" scratched on the bottom, and at the dead man's feet lay a clasp knife bearing the same initials. A neat bullet hole in the back of his skull told of the manner of Blessing's end.

As news of the find swept Barkerville, Fitzgerald instructed Sullivan to bring in Barry. But Barry had left. Very suddenly. A warrant was issued, and it was a question whether to try heading him off at Quesnel or further south at Soda Creek. Sullivan chose the latter and swung into the saddle for a ride of 120 miles.

Days later when the constable reined in his sweating mount at the Soda Creek steamboat landing, he got the baffling news that Barry had got off the sternwheeler two days before and promptly caught the six-horse stage for Yale.

It was then the quick-witted Sullivan bethought himself of

a brand new cow-country innovation, the electric telegraph. The Collins Overland Company had only just strung the wire through to Quesnel and now for the first time Soda Creek, Yale and New Westminster were in instant communication. With Sullivan looking over his shoulder, the Soda Creek operator tapped out the message that told the British Columbia Police at Yale of Barry's flight. Which, by the way, was the first time the telegraph was used in British Columbia to catch a criminal.

Twelve hours later when Barnard's stage pulled in at Yale, a police officer was waiting at the door. Barry gave a false name, protesting loudly that they had the wrong man. He ceased protesting when the cell door slammed behind him.

A wire brought Sullivan from Soda Creek.

On the journey back Barry tried to convey the idea to his escort that he'd seen two or three Chinese on the trail after he parted from Blessing near the Edwards' place. Maybe, he suggested, they had something to do with Blessing's death.

At Barkerville, following out the information supplied by Moses, the police traced Blessing's nugget pin to a dance hall girl, who said she got it from Barry. When the gambler was returned to Richfield, Fitzgerald showed him the pin and asked him if it was his.

"Sure it's mine," said Barry.

"Where did you get it?" asked the officer.

"I bought it from a man in Victoria years ago. He went back to the States," came the ready answer.

"Ever notice anything peculiar about it?" persisted the officer.

Barry suspected a trap, but couldn't fathom what it was.

"No," was the nonchalant reply. "It's just a nugget pin."

"That'll be all for the present," said Fitzgerald with just a trace of satisfaction in his tone.

It was in the summer of 1867 that Barry was led into the little courtroom at Richfield, to face that terror of mainland evil-doers, Chief Justice Matthew Baillie Begbie.

As the trial unfolded before a jury of hard-faced Cariboo miners, they heard the dovetailing evidence of Crown witnesses accounting for every movement of Barry at the end of May 1866. Finally to the witness stand came Patrick Gannon, a cattle drover, who said he'd seen Barry and Blessing eating breakfast together by a roadside fire near the Edwards' place, just a stone's throw from where the body was found.

The biggest impression was created by the Negro barber, Wellington Delaney Moses, who identified the nugget stick pin handed to him by prosecutor H. P. Walker.

How did he know it was the property of the murdered man?

Because, said Moses, when you looked at it in a certain way you could observe the profile of a man's face on one side of the nugget. Unfortunately, Blessing had told Moses, the jeweller had mounted the nugget upside down. It was the face on the nugget that Moses had momentarily spotted as he swung the sheet into position under Barry's chin! For proof, the pin was passed for inspection by judge and jury. Unmistakably they saw the face. In fact, as he held it in his left hand, Judge Begbie sketched it in his bench book.

Moses had told Fitzgerald of this tell-tale clue and Barry, questioned by the police, had fallen into the trap.

The jury said "Guilty" and at five o'clock on the morning of August 8, a gang of men could have been seen erecting a scaffold in front of the Richfield court house, about a mile from Barkerville. At seven Barry was hanged, and by eight the scaffold was gone. It was not only brief, it was also the first public execution in Richfield.

"Del" Moses continued his Barkerville barber shop for many a year after that, eventually branching out with a sideline of men's and women's wear.

The Working Man

Kim Pirie

The man works,
As the clock ticks by,
Ten cents a minute he gets,
Putting gizmos on thing-a-ma-jigs,
Two gizmos a minute,
One hundred twenty an hour,
Coffee-break, one cup of coffee,
Two cigarettes,
More gizmos, more thing-a-ma-jigs,
Day after day,
Week after week,
Month after month,
Year after year,
Life is so simple,
Why do people crack-up?

Man vs Himself

At Grips with a Grizzly
Colin Wyatt

This is the true story of probably the only man who has fought a grizzly bear with his bare hands and lived to tell the tale.

Generally you can approach most of Canada's wild animals quite safely and they pay no more attention to you than they would to another animal; their tameness is one of the joys of the great national parks of the Canadian Rockies. I have had a black bear come to the door of my cabin, accept a bowl of cookies, and walk away afterward licking his chops quite peacefully.

But the grizzly is a very different matter. They are scattered all over the Rockies, living mostly just around the tree line, and, unlike the black bear, the females go with their cubs for up to two years, thus making them already twice as potentially dangerous. The grizzly is the only animal that will go out of its way to attack human beings, not to kill and eat — its normal diet consists of berries and the rodents which it digs up — but just to maul them as a cat mauls a mouse, out of a spirit of deliberate viciousness.

Every year the papers carry a bald account of another tragedy; the details of what actually happened are generally sealed by death. But victims usually die of loss of blood and exposure, or a crushed skull.

We were sitting round the hearth one evening, talking of

grizzlies, when my friend Nick Morant, the well-known CPR photographer, pulled up his sleeve to show his terrible scars and then told me this tale:

Christian Haesler and I had gone out to take some pictures; we left from near Field at 6:30 in the morning, went up from Sherbrooke Lake near Wapta Lake. Since we were in a national park we didn't carry a rifle. We followed the trail for quite a way and we had got up above the far end of the lake near the tree line when we came on a grizzly with her cub. As we saw her she looked up at us very casual-like and Haesler said to me: "Look at that big grizzly over there!" I looked up and saw her and wasn't very worried, for I had met them before and they had never bothered me.

Haesler said: "We'll have to wait and let her make up her mind what she's going to do." She was right in the trail — so we waited and the old bear turned to her cub and they went across the creek and up toward Mt. Ogden.

Well, I figured, she'll mind her own business. She'll go her way and we'll go ours. But that's where we made our mistake — we should never have trusted her.

After we had gone along a little we looked back and there was the cub up on the mountain all by himself and no mother grizzly — then the next moment we looked over our shoulders to our left and there was mother grizzly coming after us as hard as she could come. Boy! Was she traveling!

Haesler and I threw off our rucksacks with our heavy equipment and we ran as hard as we darned well could up into the trees. Now you just go out one afternoon when you've nothing else to do and try and run up a tree as if a grizzly was after you. You've got to be up fifteen feet in fifteen seconds, and it's not very easy — go out and try some day! That's what *we* had to do.

I figured to myself that the first man to climb a tree would be the first man to get caught and if I ran further than Haesler then maybe I'd be in the clear. So that's what I did. It's not a very Christian way of thinking, perhaps, but sometimes you forget about other people and start thinking about yourself. So I ran beyond Haesler as he started up a tree — when I climbed my tree and looked back there were his legs disappearing up into the branches and, almost at the same moment, the grizzly appeared at the bottom of his tree.

She looked so small, you know, it didn't look as if she'd ever be able to get him; his legs were 'way too high. But there I was wrong. I realized then something I'd never realized before, that a bear is just like a caterpillar — you know the way a caterpillar stretches itself right out? Well, a bear does the same thing. She stood up and she took him by the leg at nine feet from the ground. She grabbed him and ripped him right out of that tree, then she jumped on him and started to tear at him.

Poor Haesler was crying for help and there was I up my tree and not knowing what to do. Now if *you* were up a tree and saw a friend being torn by a grizzly, what would *you* do? There's a real predicament; would you stay up in the tree or would you come down and try and help the other one? I really didn't know what to do, because sometimes in the bush the glorious thing to do isn't the smart thing. Maybe it's better for me to stay up here, I thought, and then, when the bear's finished mauling him, there will be someone to look after him and get help; but, on the other hand, in the meantime he's being killed. So I had quite a decision to make, for a grizzly is pretty big and you haven't much chance of coming out of it alive.

Anyway, I came down out of the tree, up behind the old grizzly, and whacked her over the backside with a stick. The grizzly didn't like that very much. She swung around and she came at me and I started to run. I was heading for Banff! Then I remembered that a grizzly can move awful fast — it can overtake a horse in an open field. So I knew if she came up behind me she would strike at me with her paws — and if you look at those rugs you'll see the size of a grizzly's paws, the claws are as big as Eversharp pencils. When a grizzly swipes at you with those claws it's like someone sticking daggers into you; just cuts you all to pieces or knocks your head off.

So I threw myself on the ground so that the bear wouldn't have a chance to strike at me with her claws and when she rushed me I kicked her in the face with my big boots.

Well, when I kicked her she got very mad. She was just as quick as lightning and grabbed my leg in her mouth. Do you feel that? Put your finger in that hole in my leg. It comes clean through the other side. The leg was split in half, just like that, quick as it takes to tell it. See the muscles here? That's where they broke through the casing. The leg was broken in two places and the muscles ripped through.

When I found the grizzly had my leg in her mouth I was very scared. I beat at her with my fists to make her let go. She let go, but then she grabbed me by the arm — see here, a cut which showed all the muscles in my arm. That rendered my arm useless and my leg useless. Then, just as quickly as she'd attacked me, she went back after the still-unconscious Haesler.

I had to get up and try to get away, but I found I had a leg broken in two places and a bad arm. I thought I'd climb a tree, but I couldn't even do that. So I just leaned against a tree. You have to remember that when you are in an accident like that, there's what the doctors call shock; you're terribly weak, you're terribly scared, you're like a little boy.

So I stood there, leaning against a tree, and, having mauled Haesler again, she came back looking for me.

Now remember that a grizzly's sight is not very good, and that I had figured the first person to climb a tree would be the first person she'd see. Well, this time she came rushing past within two feet of me — she never saw me but went rushing headlong by me. I could have touched her with my hand as she went past. She stopped about ten feet beyond me, swung around, and came back on the other side of the tree. She stood there with her behind to me and I could have reached round and touched her.

Then she must have smelled the blood on me — or more likely she must have heard me breathing, for I was breathing very heavily. So she whips around the tree and comes at me

178   Man *vs* Himself

with a hell of a roar and down I go and bite the dust again.

When she came back at me I swiped at her with my other arm and she grabbed me up here at the upper part of the elbow — she grabbed me and shook me like a rat. Have you ever seen a puppy shake a rag doll? Then she threw me about ten or fifteen feet — it felt like further — and I landed face down in a bunch of rocks. I lay there and I felt pretty sick.

Now, while all this was happening, Haesler regained consciousness and realized there was nothing he could do as he was pretty badly wounded — his arm was terribly hurt and all the muscles of his leg were exposed down to the shinbone. He made a run for it and got away. He ran and walked, and fell unconscious about eight times, all the way back to Wapta Lake. But I didn't know that, you must remember, I didn't know he'd got away.

So, after the bear had finished with me and thrown me in the rocks face down, she went back to look for Haesler. But she couldn't find him. She went rushing around in the bush looking for him and I just lay there. I could see her running around. She was so big that when she hit a tree the whole tree would shake.

I lay there and wondered what would happen — I really didn't care too much. Anyway, suddenly she came out of the brush and she makes a rush for me again. She came right at my face so I roll over and turn my face down into the rocks. She bit me all over my body — she took me by the head for eighteen stitches — she bit me behind the ear and just lifted all the side of my scalp right up. . . . (I remember everything very well; I didn't get unconscious or anything like that — at least, I don't think I did.)

Then she stepped on me once, just like somebody putting a grand piano on me, a terrible weight. She walked right clean over me and past me, over to where the trail was.

I looked up and there was the cub; he'd come down from the mountainside. That cub saved my life.

But I was very annoyed, for I always believed that if you

left animals alone they'd leave you alone — and so they will, except for the grizzly who is very unpredictable.

I swore at Mother Bear, called her every name under the sun; told her to go home.

And then she started at me a fourth time. Just as she came at me the cub let out a little yelping noise, she turned around and went off down the trail with the cub.

Now you may think that's the end of the story, but it isn't. It took Haesler about six hours to get out — he didn't get down until late in the afternoon.

Now you must remember that the bear went off down the trail between me and civilization and left me blocked up in a canyon. But I believed that Haesler was still there; but he wasn't, he was on his way out. So I figured I'd have to go and get help. I worried about him so I went to look for him as best I could with a broken leg in two places. I couldn't find him, so there was only one thing to do and that was to go and get help, and, to get help I had to go out *behind* the bear; if I went down the trail I'd run into the bear again.

There was only one thing to do and that was to circle the area; in other words go all around where I thought the bear was. The mountains there are very steep and I had to go and look for a way out. I had to cross the creek, and I marked my trail with my windbreaker so they would know where to look when they came looking for Haesler.

I climbed nearly two thousand feet up Mt. Ogden with my broken leg, right up to the snow line, walked all day and climbed down to the shores of Sherbrooke Lake, and there *I* found the people going out to look for *me*. I had been eleven hours out with no help at all — the blood was clotted three inches deep on my shoulder, and the first man I met fainted at the sight of me. I had a very bad time of it.

Both Haesler and I lived to tell the story, but he died a year or two later from a heart attack. I was in hospital a long time, but I've now completely recovered.

Ladysmith's Death Watch
T. W. Paterson

Sunday, Oct. 5, 1979, will mean little out of the ordinary to most Vancouver Island residents. But to oldtimers of Ladysmith it is a date to be remembered: The 70th anniversary of the day 32 men — and a town's dreams — died.

The fateful Tuesday had dawned over the Wellington Collieries at Extension like most October mornings, grey and wet. As they had so many times before, the morning shift had clambered aboard the train at Ladysmith to puff a winding 20 miles to No. 2 Mine. Here, amid coal-grimed sheds squatting on the cliffside, a mile-long slope descended into the mountain's belly, branching off into a network of levels and stalls which joined No. 1 and No. 3 shafts.

First word of tragedy reached Ladysmith at 9 a.m., when a telephone call breathlessly announced engineer McKay was steaming down at full speed for medical assistance and company officials.

The news spread instantly. Within minutes, men, women and children had swarmed to the station for word of husband, father and son with the morning shift.

Officials forbade any passengers on the return trip as relief crews had already been organized at the mines, remembering the explosion of eight years before when a wave of over-eager rescuers had charged in to the mines, driving fleeing miners back into the dreaded afterdamp, and 16 had died.

When McKay screeched to a stop in the crowded stations, a deathless silence descended upon the pensive throng. The crew quietly stated the explosion had occurred in No. 3 level, that not more than 14 men could have been involved.

The hours ticked painfully by for those waiting. Few spoke. Only an occasional child's cry or a dog's whining broke the stillness. Then a telephone message raised the number of missing to 20. At 4 o'clock, they were told 31 men had been entombed.

Three and a half hours later, McKay brought down the first load of bodies.

"Many who had been anxiously awaiting to hear from father, brother or son were now brought face to face with the fate of the missing one," reported *The Colonist*. "The scenes were pathetic, especially at the homes where small children were deprived suddenly of a father.

"The first train down with the bodies reached Ladysmith yard at 7:30 in the evening, and there was a great crowd here to assist in the work of moving the dead to their respective homes. The bodies brought in were those of Edward Dunn, William Davidson, Thos. O'Connell, Andrew Moffatt, James Molyneux, Thomas Thomas and one other.

"As each body was passed off on a stretcher the name was called out and some relative or the representatives of the secret society to which the dead belonged took charge of the body. It was an impressive scene."

The trainmen had orders to return the stretchers for the next shipment.

By the time it was known the explosion had occurred in levels 2½ and 3 of No. 2 mine, 18 bodies had been recovered.

At Extension's Tunnel Hotel, Thomas Hislop, one of the last of 700 miners to reach safety, gave a vivid account of his escape. Of the seven men in his crew, working in No. 4 west level at 8:30 a.m., only he and one other had survived.

The muffled explosion had been followed by a great rush of air, he said. "Bob White, he drops his pick and shouts, 'My God, she's blasted!'

"We stood still for a second in the darkness. The rush of wind put our lamps out until someone comes with a safety lamp."

With the precious lamp had been another party of 16. Grabbing hold of each other's coattails, the terrified men had shuffled through the eerie darkness, following the glistening rails in their solitary beacon's feeble glow.

They had stumbled but a short distance when a "great cloud of smoke blew into our faces," said Hislop, "and we got a whiff of afterdamp and knew we must go back.

"Through into the counter level we went, but we couldn't get through. The damp drives us out, back into the level again. We tried to clamber up in No. 10 stall, across to the crosscut, but were driven out."

The macabre dance of death seemed endless. "In No. 3 counter level we left five men. . . . When we lost them we did not know the damp had got them. We knew nothing then except that the smoke and damp was chasing us whichever way we went. We struggled on through a while, being most lost."

Then, there in the lethal darkness, the dead, dying and gas all about them, Hislop and comrades had held desperate counsel. "We were tired and beaten back. The firedamp came so thick that it couldn't be faced, and we had to run back from it."

Exhausted, surrounded by afterdamp and lost, the 17 had decided to remain where they were. They were trapped. They could do nothing but wait — and pray.

"We had not waited long when we heard a shout, and Alex Shaw, the foreman, and Davidson — him as lost his son in the mine — came. When we heard their shouts, instructing us, we smashed through the stopping and crawled over to safety. Then fatigued and worn out, we climbed out up the slope, clinging to each other's coattails, helped by men, who met us with safety lanterns."

At the entrance, Hislop and company had waited for their five missing comrades. "But (they) never came out, and I'm waiting still for them. They must have been dead a long while now, though."

That night, *The Colonist* reported, Ladysmith awaited its dead, "a sad, grief-stricken community. From the time the telephone message gave the first brief bulletin of the disaster this morning, and the train came down the hill from the mine to take doctors and rescuers, sorrow has followed upon sorrow.

"The bereaved men and relatives are being kept back from the mines, and the officials are keeping silent. But at intervals news comes that causes agonizing shrieks in a miner's home."

When the train from Victoria arrived, the tragedy deepened. One young passenger, told a third brother had perished in the mine, was carried "wailing bitterly up the hill". She had come from Kansas to visit. Behind her a girl met by her father screamed hysterically.

"These are the scenes such as Ladysmith has witnessed all day."

Rescue operations had begun immediately after No. 2 had been evacuated. Those who made it to the surface in the first few minutes after the blast lived; then only the dead remained.

Foreman Alex Shaw had immediately called for volunteers. Crews then had risked the poisonous afterdamp to clear away rubble and repair ventilation systems as others roamed the killing darkness in search of bodies and, hopefully, survivors.

Provincial inspectors of mines, H. F. Shepherd and Archibald Dick, hurried from Nanaimo with senior company officials to supervise operations and examine No. 2 for continuing signs of explosion. A cursory examination disclosed structural damage to be surprisingly slight, with but "comparatively few of the timbers blown out, and but one or two caves, where the roofing has fallen. One obstruction of about 50 feet with a good deal of fallen coal stopped the work of those searching for bodies near midnight, when 18 had been recovered."

The scenes which had greeted rescuers underground defied description. The miners worked in choking fumes without thinking. There would be time enough to think — and shudder — later.

First body recovered was that of popular Ladysmith vocalist James Molyneux, followed shortly by that of Tom Hislop's ill-fated companion Bob White. He had refused to leave James Ismaster and was found with his arm about his "butty". Their three fallen companions, even in death, held the preceding man's coattail.

White's brother-in-law, football star Tom O'Connell, had been found shortly after. Told of the loss of husband and brother, Mrs. White, mother of six, collapsed.

Young Fred Ingham, whose sister had been told of his fate upon arriving from Victoria, was the third brother lost in mining accidents. Mrs. Dougherty mourned her third husband killed underground.

Most bodies showed no sign of injury, indicating they had been overcome by afterdamp when fleeing, they were found pitched forward, hands over their faces in a vain attempt to ward off the pervading gas. Montenegrin Alex Melos and another miner had suffered fractured skulls, apparently having tumbled down a crosscut during their flight.

The force of the explosion had thrown young Eddie Dunn between the wheels of his cart. Amazingly, his mule, Bess, had escaped, to terrify rescue workers when she galloped madly through the smoke, a grey apparition.

As in all disasters, fate had played its harrowing game of chance at Extension. John Wargo and fellow Croatian James Kesserich had returned the night before from a hunting trip to Wolf Mountain. They had originally intended to hunt another day but, sadly, had changed their minds at the last minute and returned to work. Kesserich had planned to work just a week longer, then return to his homeland where he had bought a farm.

Hermann Peterson's wife had died a month before; they left five orphans.

Ladysmith Mayor D. Nicholson and MP Ralph Smith cut short visits to Victoria and hurried back to the grief-stricken community.

The tragedy was felt keenly in Victoria where many of Extension's victims had relatives and friends. Tom O'Connell and young Ingham were best known, the latter because his brother had died in hospital here from an accident in the mines just a short time before.

Said *The Colonist:* "Those are fortunate who have never realized the horror which the people of a mining community experience when a disaster such as this takes place. The memory of it is never forgotten, and the dread of its recurrence is seldom absent from the minds of the wives and mothers, as they part with their loved ones when the hour comes for the workers to go down into the mine.

"But if we cannot fully comprehend the terrible suspense and anxiety of the poor women of Ladysmith, we can offer them our sympathy in their grief for the loss of their husbands and sons."

The dangerous task of recovering the dead continued throughout the night, as Inspectors Shepherd and Dick gingerly probed rubble amid the threat of gas to determine the extent of damages and cause of the blast. Most miners agreed it had occurred as the result of a carelessly placed charge in No. 22 stall of Wargo, Kesserich and John Bullitch, although Shepherd expressed doubts.

By the following morning, all but two bodies had been recovered, relief parties suffering intensely from exhaustion and lingering gas.

At the surface, the rest of the ill-fated morning shift waited for word of brother, son and comrade. Hour by hour they waited. Small groups numbly conjectured as to what had happened, but most stood silently, stubbing their boots against the rails and smoking.

Periodically, the flickering headlight of an ore wagon would round a curve a mile down the slope and slowly approach the pithead. No one spoke as heads strained eagerly, yet fearfully, for a glimpse of a canvas-shrouded form. Then the pathetic shape would be identified and a husky miner, tears streaking his blackened face, would stumble away.

Earlier, they had been excited by the rumor, "There's someone alive!"

"Well," rejoined another hopefully, "if a mule could get out there's a chance."

"He's behind a 12-foot wall but they heard him and are getting in to him!" cried a third.

But the mystery voice had been that of a rescuer, separated from his party. The death watch continued.

When all were accounted for, 32 good men were dead.

Survivors told tales of miraculous escape. David Irving had "gone to the counter level from the main level, where I had been working, when I heard the shock, light at first, but the rush of wind which followed put out my naked light.

"I had a safety lamp at the face and when the man who had been working in the counter level came we went together and got my lamp. Then Davidson came and said to get him but when we came to his place he had gone. We picked up A. Dewar and we all tried to get to the main level, but the damp growing hotter beat us back. We went back to where we came from and were joined by Tom Hislop's party. We all made our way to No. 4 level and sat there. There were two safety lamps in the party and with those leading we tried to counter but were beat again by the damp.

"We tried to clamber up the hill to No. 12 stall, but there came a rush of wind and damp through the crosscut that put my lamp out. We thought the end had come and went back, gradually forced by the gas, until we came to a place where there was some air and sat down. We had given up and were talking. It was this talking that saved us. The Shaws and Davidson heard our talk and they broke off a board from the stopping and let us through to safety."

The tales of bitter coincidence increased with each passing hour, someone recalling the ironic twist which had condemned a comrade to horrifying death in the darkness. Someone said young Quinn's mother had lost two husbands in the mine and another son but a few months earlier. Thomas Thomas had escaped a mine disaster some years before which had claimed the life of his father.

Negro Jerry Lewis had been reported lost when a body, face charred black by firedamp, was found. Lewis had immediately reported himself alive and well. Two other miners said they had been at work at the estimated site of the blast but minutes before.

Mrs. Mansell had been driving along Seattle's Second Avenue with her husband when they heard a newsboy shouting "all about the mine disaster at Nanaimo". As Mr. Mansell had several friends in the Nanaimo mines, he had bought a copy.

"The first name I saw was that of my brother," said the grieving visitor.

Extension's No. 2 had long been regarded as safe; unlike No. 1 and 3, this was a "naked light" mine where openflame lamps, cigarettes and matches were permitted.

Ladysmith then turned to burying her dead. The bodies lying in sacks under a snow shed at Extension were shipped to their homes when coffins were rushed in from Victoria.

Within a week, No. 2 was again in production but, ultimately, Oct. 5, 1909 proved to be more than a day of horror and death. For booming coal town Ladysmith, then enjoying high hopes of a bustling future, it meant near ruin. Bitter labor disputes and vanishing markets haunted the little town on the 49th parallel in following years. Then the stock market plunge of 1929 delivered the final blow to Extension's once-roaring mines which had yielded 1,600 tons of black gold a day.

The Trapper

Colleen deJong

The even rhythm of snow shoes crunching on the frozen snow stopped as the trapper halted momentarily to adjust a pack that had become loose on the sled. Shading his eyes with his hand, he gazed at his surroundings. The gleaming white snow lay peacefully about him. Far off in the clear sky, a flock of birds could be seen. A cold Arctic wind made him pull the hood of his parka closer around his face. Once more, he started on his way.

"Sam always was a fool anyways," the trapper suddenly muttered out loud. "It's not surprising that he got eaten by some wild animal. The fellows back at camp got all crazy when they found him, or what was left of him. They called it revenge. Ha! No dumb animal could ever get revenge. I always said he was too soft to be a trapper in the first place. Sam, I used to say, it doesn't make no difference to the animal how you kill it."

He walked on in silence for a few moments. Again he spoke out loud as though he was talking to someone nearby.

"Even that dog of his was a fool," he went on. "That ugly mongrel he called a full bred husky was scared of anything that moved. Sam used to treat that animal like it was his only friend. Made him that fancy leather collar and everything. All that fuss over some dumb animal."

The trapper paused briefly to catch his breath and then continued. "There was no sign of that dog when the fellows found Sam. No doubt that wild animal they ran into made a good meal out of him. Well, that's what you get for being a softy. Revenge, ha! They're all crazy!"

He let out a sad sigh and shook his head from side to side. Without saying anything else, he trudged on in silence through the deep snow.

Not long afterwards, the trapper came upon the beginning of a long rocky ridge. Here he found the first trap of his trap line. The sharp steel jaws of the trap were closed upon the front paws of a small Arctic fox. In an effort to free itself, the animal had tried to gnaw off its paws. The dead fox lay in a mess of blood-stained snow.

When the trapper saw his prize, his face quickly spread into a wide grin. This beauty would certainly get him a nice sum. He walked over to the trap and carefully removed the fox. Its fur was frozen into the bloody snow and it took some time for him to free the pelt without damaging it. He tied the fox onto his sled and headed for the next trap.

Within the following hours, the trapper had reached several more of his traps. So far, only one had failed to produce anything. The sled, with its increasing load, was becoming more and more difficult to pull through the snow-covered rocks.

At one point, the man stopped to rest in a hollow formed by two high ridges. From the pack on his sled, he removed a small package containing dried meat. This he proceeded to eat while sitting on the edge of the sled. He had not been there long, when suddenly he felt his muscles tighten. Something was watching him! The trapper jumped to his feet and flung around. He could see only the snow-covered rocks. Then from somewhere behind the hollow, came the sound of snow falling loose from a cliff. He grabbed for the loaded rifle on the sled and stood waiting. Nothing appeared. The trapper felt ashamed when he suddenly found himself shivering. Surely it was only from the cold. He returned the package back to its place in the sled, but kept the gun cradled in the crook of his arm. Slowly he pulled the sled out of the hollow. What had been there? Was it only his imagination? For some reason, the trapper couldn't help remembering Sam. Deep in the back of his mind, he heard Sam shout, "Revenge!"

Dusk began to settle over the cold white land. Dim northern lights flickered across the deep blue sky. The trapper, now very weary, came upon a place in the ridge where a wide river intersected it. Since the river was covered with snow, it was difficult to tell where the bank began. Being careful to stay far away from the river, which might not be completely frozen, he pulled the sled close along the ridge. The man left the sled and walked between the rocks. Soon he came to a place where a pile of bushes were stacked high against a steep wall. Carefully the trapper removed the bushes. The mouth of a short but wide cave was revealed. The trapper cautiously checked to make sure the cave was uninhabited and then returned to the sled. He dragged it as close as possible to the cave and removed his pack. To safeguard the sled from any wild animals, he then placed the bushes over top of it.

Next he built a fire in front of the cave. Taking his pack and his gun with him, he retreated into the cave for the evening. Again he took some food from his pack and ate it ravenously while staring into the fire. Not far off, a lone wolf was howling. Suddenly, from outside, the rustling of bushes could be heard. The trapper immediately bolted up and grabbed for his gun. He sat motionless, peering out into the dark. The noise could no longer be heard, but he dared not move. The fire in front of him slowly began to die. Totally filled with fear, he sat paralyzed, staring out into the night.

The trapper suddenly spotted a movement. Madly he began to fire the rifle. Before he realized what was happening, he used up all of his bullets. He dropped his rifle and sat waiting. For what, he didn't know. Two shiny white eyes appeared out of the dark. Horrified, the trapper began to whisper, "Revenge, it wants revenge." Completely overtaken by panic, he fled out of the cave and ran screaming down towards the river. Before he knew it, he was on the ice. Suddenly the ice gave way and the trapper was pulled under the icy swirling water.

A limping dog approached the edge of the river. It was wearing a handmade leather collar. The husky lifted its muzzle to the sky, and let out a deep lonely howl for the trapper he wanted to be friends with.

Watch the Fires Burn

Samuel Roddan

On Wednesday everybody at school had a half-holiday because Mr. McGlashan, the principal, was holding a meeting with the teachers to discuss how they could get more money for their work. It was too hot for fishing at Three Mile Creek, and besides we didn't have any worms, so instead, Benny and I hopped on our bikes and pedalled through sleepy Pine Park to the waterfront.

"We'll visit Uncle Paddy; that's what we'll do," Benny said as he whizzed along. And making noises like McGregor's big six-wheel truck, we pumped down Waverley, past the old school and the Baptist Church to the corner of Main. Near Rodger's drug store we shouted at Mr. Campbell, the barber, who was standing outside his shop reading the *Chronicle:*

"Mr. Campbell shaves your head,
Before he toddles home to bed,
Oh, Mr. Campbell shaves your head
And so he will until he's dead."

"Around again," Benny yelled and we circled fast and gave the second verse to Mr. Campbell, who shook his fist at us, which was what we wanted, and then we headed for the docks and the shingle mill owned by Benny's Uncle Paddy.

At the top of Waterfront Hill we leaned back on our bike seats, and riding free-hand, looked over the dark, blue ocean water, past the scraggy old jack pine on Rock Peak, to the smoky hills of Vancouver Island rolling through the mist like giant porpoises. And then we breathed in all the wonderful tide smells floating up from the ocean — the raw, sweet smells of cedar and the musty perfume of freshly sawn lumber — and far below we could see the tin roofs of the shingle mill, the smoke from the sawdust burner, and Uncle Paddy's men dancing across the log booms with their long, shiny pike poles.

At the mill gate Uncle Paddy was bossing his men and showing them how they should do their job, but when he saw us he butted his cigar and snapped his bright red braces with his thumbs.

"Why sure," he said, "this ain't a Saturday, but I'll show you the mill. You gaffers are lucky we're not busy today. Come on." And walking with Uncle Paddy into the great noisy shed made us feel big and important for he only had to lift an eyebrow to make his men hop to it.

Uncle Paddy hoisted us up on the loading platform, and we watched the logs moving along the slip to the bull saw. A colored man with bulging muscles and blood-shot eyes smashed at them with his hammer, and each log groaned as it hit the saw and left a stream of spurting gray-red sawdust. Then Uncle Paddy pointed his finger at the bobbing heads of the Chinese men in the deep cellar far below the log deck.

"As I've always said, they're the best workers I've got in the mill," Uncle Paddy shouted. "Look at 'em go."

Benny and I stared down through the dust at the Chinese men packing the shingles in little bundles, jabbering and yelling and going to beat sixty to earn their money. Every now and then a great cloud of steam, which Uncle Paddy said was to control the dust, swept over them so that we saw only their heads floating in waves of fog, and sometimes we could see their arms, and it looked as though they were drowning swimmers, catching at straws and bobbing up and down for the last time.

A big man with bushy eyebrows, a white shirt, and a diamond stickpin in his tie scrambled onto the loading platform beside us. His sleeves were rolled up and his thick arms were covered with bristly, black hairs and he was breathing and puffing hard. He shook his fat finger in the air and then he waved his finger up and down at Uncle Paddy and started to yell: "Who are these kids?" and "If things don't speed up in this crazy mill, I'll fire the whole caboodle." And I guess it was then, when I saw Uncle Paddy turning white and rubbing at his face and saying, "Yes, sir; yes, Mr. Rabsky," that I suddenly figured Uncle Paddy wasn't the big boss after all.

Benny was staring with his mouth open at Uncle Paddy, then he gave me the high sign and we made ourselves scarce and beat it over to the burner, where all the sawdust came.

"I thought Uncle Paddy was the big boss," I said to Benny as we hurried along, keeping an eye out for Mr. Rabsky.

"Well, he must have just sold the mill to Mr. Rabsky last week," Benny said sadly, "or else Uncle Paddy owns it only on Saturdays when Mr. Rabsky isn't around. But it's about the same as with your Pop. He doesn't own the church he preaches in, you know."

"My Pop is the boss in his church on Sundays," I said loyally.

"But there's no real difference, when you come to think of it," Benny said, trying to change the subject from Pop, for I knew I had him there. "You have to consider all the freedom Uncle Paddy has to walk about and snap his braces and give orders and run the place when Mr. Rabsky's gone. It's just as good as being boss."

Joe, the night watchman, said "Hello" and we watched him working on the furnace. Joe lived in a little shack behind the office. Some people said he was the richest man in town and that his mattress was stuffed with ten dollar bills, but we didn't know that for sure. Most of the time Joe sat on a little bench beside the furnace, rubbing at the place his thumb used to be, smoking his pipe, and sometimes he would get up and check the dampers.

"Stand back and watch her from the side or she'll make a cinder of you if she blows," Joe said, as we crowded into the furnace room.

Then Joe unbolted the white-hot door and we squinted into the fire and watched the sawdust pouring in a golden stream into the burner where it burst up like flashing stars of flame.

"Nuff heat to roast all the heathen of the waterfront," Joe said proudly.

"I bet it's a million times hotter than the hot place." Benny said, sucking in his lips. And watching the flames roaring and dancing, licking the red-white bricks and bursting from the mouth of the furnace, we were remembering the long, long sermons in Pop's church about the everlasting fires.

"There's heat for you," Joe said as he pulled the big lever to shut the fire door. "Now, boys. Listen to her roar."

The furnace groaned in hunger like an Indian elephant, and above its deep-throated bellows we could hear the whine and piercing moan of the saws tearing through the logs. Then Mr. Rabsky suddenly came in the door and behind him was Uncle Paddy, his face still white, and it looked as though he were trying to hide it with his hand.

Mr. Rabsky looked at Benny and me and his red face started to swell up and just when it seemed he was about to grab us by the pants, the furnace gave a great grumble and roar and the flames licked out of the draft openings as though they were trying to get at Mr. Rabsky.

"Watch that furnace!" Mr. Rabsky bellowed, jumping back.

"You'll have us in ashes one of these days."

"It's all right, Mr. Rabsky," Joe said, rubbing at the place his thumb used to be. And he touched the draft levers here and there like he was playing an organ and soon the big furnace quietened down and began to purr gently as if it were a kitten tickled behind the ears. Mr. Rabsky glared at the furnace and at Benny and me, and because he couldn't stand the heat very well, he puffed his cheeks a couple of times and spat on the floor and went out.

"You kids run off now," Uncle Paddy said over his shoulder. "We're very busy today." Uncle Paddy's face twitched a little as he shuffled after Mr. Rabsky and he seemed bent over and tired looking and he was not snapping his braces the way he did most of the time on a Saturday.

One night about nine o'clock Benny and I were sitting on my front porch. We had just got back from Scouts and were trying to count how many stars there are in the Milky Way, practising for the Astronomer's Badge, which is one of the toughest to win. We were up to sixty-eight when we heard the fire engines.

"Could be a whopper," I shouted hopefully.

"Sure sounds like a dandy," Benny said and we automatically grabbed our bikes and wheeled fast out of the yard.

For a while Benny didn't say anything more because he was bent double over the handlebars for speed, and then McGregor's truck roared past us loaded with the Volunteer Fire Brigade, including Mr. Campbell, the barber, hanging on to his helmet and yelling to Mr. McGregor to slow down for Mr. Rodger at the drug store.

"Oh, Mr. Campbell shaves your head,
And so he will until he's dead."

Benny shouted, and after I had caught up to him on Main Street and straightened up to ride the seat for a minute, we saw the whole sky above the waterfront bursting into a great ball of fire and we knew right away it was Uncle Paddy's shingle mill, only of course, it really belonged to Mr. Rabsky.

Soon we began to feel the heat of the fire on our faces and in the brightness of the flames it was clear as day. Chunks of ash sailed like kites over the buildings and when they drifted to earth the Chinese men who worked in the mill pounced on them, shouting and screaming, and beat them into tiny puffs of powder; but two of the Chinese were sitting on the sidewalk with their heads buried in their hands wailing like they do at a funeral and Uncle Paddy was running everywhere trying to count and see if any of his workers were missing.

Benny and I ditched our bikes where they were safe and ran

across Mill Bridge which was covered with the hoses stretching out like snakes to the fire hydrants on Front Street. Then we saw Mr. McGregor, who was Fire Chief of the Volunteers, with the badge of two axes on his helmet, waving his arms and yelling at his men. Benny and I wriggled through the crowd, and from behind the big, red Pumper which the Volunteer Fire Brigade had just bought last month, we watched the flames bouncing and crackling into the sky.

And now Benny and I cheered on the brave fire fighters and at the same time prayed the flames might grow brighter and taller and fiercer. And remembering Mr. Rabsky we hoped for a mighty explosion that would send sheets of fire miles into the sky. And thinking of Uncle Paddy and visits that would be no more, we cursed the slowness of the fire fighters and helped with the hoses and dragged at them the way Mr. Campbell was doing. Once when we looked around we saw Mr. Rabsky pacing up and down and giving orders and wringing his big hands. Then Uncle Paddy and Mr. Rodger came running by with an empty fire hose uncurling behind them. Suddenly the water spurted out, and the nozzle waved back and forth, jerked from their hands, and thrashed on the ground with the great spurts of water spraying and shooting over the crowd. Before you could say "Jack Robinson", Mr. Rabsky let go with a string of swear words and jumped from behind the Pumper and started to crawl on his hands and knees toward the nozzle.

"It'll kill you," Uncle Paddy shouted, but Mr. Rabsky kept moving along the wriggling hose, and when he slowed down he watched the thumping nozzle like a cat does a mouse, his head going from side to side and his back curved ready to spring. Suddenly Mr. Rabsky bounced forward and rolled over and over, and when he staggered to his feet the hose tossed him around like a dancer and blood oozed from his face but the nozzle was clenched tight in his hands with the water pouring into the flames. Step by step Mr. Rabsky pulled the hose forward and we could almost see the veins standing out on his neck as he kept pushing the great stream of water toward the office, which was where, I guess, he kept all his money. Then a billow of smoke covered him up and all we could see was the hose jerking ahead and the water slashing through the flames, knocking the shingles from the blazing roof. After a long while the hose stopped moving and the smoke lifted a little, and Mr. Rabsky came reeling back, still holding the hose with the water spurting at the flames, and half under his arm was a great soggy bundle which we knew in a moment was Joe, the night watchman.

Four men, including Uncle Paddy and Mr. Campbell, ran up and grabbed the hose from Mr. Rabsky, who bent over and threw Joe on his shoulder and tottered back like a drunken man to the Pumper. Somebody whose name I didn't know took Joe from Mr. Rabsky and laid him gently on the ground and then Major Davidson, who is in charge of the Salvation Army in our town, rushed up with a blanket and a steaming pot of coffee. Mr. Rabsky pulled the blanket around Joe and flopped on his knees and started to press on Joe's back with his hands, doing it slowly and carefully and counting it out the way it has to be done; but every now and then he looked into Joe's face and shook his head. Finally, Major Davidson kneeled down beside Joe as though he was going to offer up a prayer, but instead he held a tiny mirror to Joe's mouth and when it misted over with moisture from his feeble breath, Major Davidson lifted his eyes to Heaven; but Mr. Rabsky kept at his job harder than ever.

Now everybody was pushing forward and shouting, "Get back and give him air," so Benny and I helped Uncle Paddy hold the mob in a big circle so that Joe could breathe in all the fresh air he needed. Suddenly Joe's legs started to kick and he coughed and spluttered. Then, for the first time, Mr. Rabsky took it easy and leaned back on his heels, and not noticing the coffee in Major Davidson's hand and which had cooled off anyway, he pulled a shiny, silver bottle from his pocket. First

Mr. Rabsky took a long, slow drink himself, and after it had gurgled down he bent over and poured the rest into Joe's mouth. Joe sat up quick, rubbed at the place his thumb used to be, and started to babble and smile.

And now Mr. Rabsky got to his feet, and everybody, including the Chinese men and Benny and I, let go with three cheers and a tiger. Uncle Paddy and Mr. Campbell rushed up to pat Mr. Rabsky on the back, but he shrugged them away and instead he kept busy dusting off his hands and wiping the sweat from his face. And after he had cinched up his trousers, straightened his tie, and put on his hat, which Benny had found under the right wheel of the Pumper, Mr. Rabsky pushed his way through the crowd, not saying anything and not looking back but just walking by himself across Mill Bridge into the darkness of the town.

The Skating Party
Merna Summers

Our house looked down on the lake. From the east windows you could see it: a long sickle of blue, its banks hung with willow. Beyond was a wooded ridge, which, like all such ridges in our part of the country, ran from northeast to southwest.

In another part of the world, both lake and ridge would have had names. Here, only people had names. I was Maida; my father was Will, my mother was Winnie. Take us all together and we were the Singletons. The Will Singletons, that is as opposed to the Dan Singletons, who were my grandparents and dead, or Nathan Singleton, who was my uncle and lived in the city.

In the books I read, lakes and hills had names, and so did ponds and houses. Their names made them more real to me, of greater importance, than the hills and lakes and sloughs that

I saw every day. I was eleven years old before I learned that the hill on which our house was built had once had a name. It was called Stone Man Hill. My parents had never thought to tell me that.

It was my uncle, Nathan Singleton, who told me. Uncle Nathan was a bachelor. He had been a teacher before he came to Willow Bunch, but he had wanted to be a farmer. He had farmed for a few years when he was a young man, on a quarter that was now part of our farm. His quarter was just south of what had been my grandfather's home place, and was now ours. But then he had moved to the city and become a teacher again.

In some ways it seemed as if he had never really left Willow Bunch. He spent all his holidays at our place, taking walks with me, talking to my mother, helping my father with such chores as he hadn't lost the knack of performing. Our home was his home. I found it hard to imagine him as I knew he must be in his classroom: wearing a suit, chalk dust on his sleeve, putting seat work on the blackboard. He didn't even talk like a teacher.

Uncle Nathan was older than my father, quite a lot older, but he didn't seem so to me. In some ways he seemed younger, for he told me things and my father did not. Not that my father was either silent or unloving. He talked as much as anybody, and he was fond of some people — me included — and showed it. What he did not give away was information.

Some children are sensitive: an eye and ear and a taking-in of subtleties. I wasn't like that. I wanted to be told. I wanted to know how things really were and how people really acted. Sometimes it seemed to me that collecting the facts was uphill work. I persisted because it was important to me to have them. I wanted to know who to praise and who to blame. Until I was in my mid-teens, that didn't seem to me to be too much to ask.

Perhaps my father had a reluctance to look at things too closely himself. He wanted to like people, and he may have found it easier to do if he kept them a little out of focus. Besides that, he believed that life was something that children should be protected from knowing about for as long as possible.

I got most of my information from my mother. She believed that knowledge was protection: that children had a right to know and parents had an obligation to teach. She didn't know all there was to know, but what she did know she intended to pass on to me.

I knew this because I heard her say so one night after I had gone to bed. Uncle Nathan, who was at the farm for the weekend, saw things my mother's way.

"What you don't know *can* hurt you," he said. "Especially what you don't know about yourself."

So my mother and my uncle talked to me, both as a sort of innoculation against life and because, I now believe, both of them liked to talk anyway. I was always willing to listen. My father listened too. He might feel that my mother told me too much, but his conviction wasn't strong enough to stop her.

It was Uncle Nathan, talking for pleasure, not policy, who gave me the pleasure of knowing that I lived in a place with a name. Stone Man Hill was so named, he said, because long ago there had existed on the slopes below our house the shape of a man, outlined in fieldstones.

"He was big," Uncle Nathan said. "Maybe fifteen yards, head to foot."

It was a summer afternoon. I was eleven. My father, in from the fields for coffee, was sitting at the kitchen table. His eyelashes were sooty with field dust. My mother was perched on a kitchen stool by the cupboard, picking over berries.

"He must have been quite a sight," my father said.

I walked to the east window of the kitchen and looked out, trying to imagine our hillside field of brome as unbroken prairie sod, trying to picture what a stone man would look like stretched out among the buffalo beans and gopher holes, his face to the sky.

"You get me a writing pad and I'll show you what he looked like," Uncle Nathan said.

I got the pad and Uncle Nathan sat down at the table

opposite my father. I sat beside him, watching as he began to trace a series of dots. His hands worked quickly, as if the dots were already visible, but only to his eyes. The outline of a man took shape.

"Who made the stone man?" I asked.

"Indians," Uncle Nathan said. He held the picture up, as if considering additions. "But I don't know when and I don't know why."

"He could have been there a hundred years," my father said. "Maybe more. There was no way of telling."

"I used to wonder why the Indians chose this hill," Uncle Nathan said. "I still do."

He got up and walked to the window, looking out at the hill and the lake and the ridge. "It may be that it was some sort of holy place to them," he said.

My mother left the cupboard and came across to the table. She picked up Uncle Nathan's drawing. Looking at it, the corners of her mouth twitched upwards.

"You're sure you haven't forgotten anything?" she asked. "Your mother used to say that the stone man was very complete."

Uncle Nathan returned her smile. "The pencil's right here, Winnie," he said. "You're welcome to it."

My father spoke quickly. "It was too bad the folks didn't have a camera," he said. "It would have been nice to have a picture of the stone man."

My mother went back to her berries.

"I've always been sorry I was too young to remember him," my father said. "Before he turned into a rock pile, that is."

I hadn't yet got around to wondering about the stone man's disappearance. Now I did. He should still have been on the hillside for me to look at. My father had been a baby when his people came to Willow Bunch, and he couldn't remember the stone man. My uncle had been a young man and could. But the difference in their ages and experience hadn't kept them from sharing a feeling of excitement at the thought of a stone man on our hillside. Why had my grandfather been insensible to this appeal? Hadn't he liked the stone man?

"Liking wouldn't enter into it," my father said.

"Your grandfather had a family to feed. He knew where his duty lay."

"There was 30 acres broke when Pa bought this place," Uncle Nathan said. "He thought he needed more. And this hill was the only land he could break without brushing it first."

Somebody else had owned our place before my grandfather, hadn't they? I asked. He hadn't turned the stone man into a rock pile.

"He was a bachelor," my father said.

"The way your grandfather saw it," Uncle Nathan said, "it was a case of wheat or stones. And he chose wheat."

"Which would you have chosen?" I asked Uncle Nathan. "Which did you want?"

"I wanted both," Uncle Nathan said.

"The choice wasn't yours to make." My mother spoke as if she were defending him.

"That's what I thought then," Uncle Nathan said.

"I thought when Pa told me to get those rocks picked, that that was what I had to do. I think now I should have spoken up. I know for years I felt guilty whenever I remembered that I had done just what was expected of me."

He looked up, a half-smile on his face. "I know it sounds crazy," he said, "but I felt as if the stone man had more claim on me than my own father did."

"We all of us think some crazy things sometimes," my father said.

From my point of view, Uncle Nathan had only one peculiarity. He had never married. And though I sometimes asked him why, I never found any satisfaction in his answers.

"Maybe it wasn't every girl who took my eye," he told me

once. "I'd pity the girl who had to count on me to take care of her," he said another time.

Then my mother told me about the skating party. It had been a dark night in November, and my mother, five years old, had come to our lake with her parents, and spent the night pushing a kitchen chair in front of her across the ice, trying to learn to skate. The party was being held in honour of Uncle Nathan and a girl called Eunice Lathem. They were to be married soon, and their friends planned, after the skating to go up to the house and present a gift to them. The gift and the fact that the party was in her honour were to be a surprise to Eunice. Nathan, for some reason, had been told about it.

There had been cold that year but no snow, so you could skate all over the lake. My mother remembered them skimming by, the golden lads and girls who made up the world when she was small, and Nathan and Eunice the most romantic of all. Nathan was handsome and Eunice was beautiful and they were very much in love, she said.

She remembered the skaters by moonlight, slim black shapes mysterious against the silver fields. There were a lot of clouds in the sky that night and when the moon went behind one of them, friends, neighbours and parents' friends became alike: all equally unknown, unidentifiable.

My grandfather and Uncle Nathan had built a big wood fire at the near end of the lake. My mother said that it was a grand experience to skate off into the darkness and the perils and dangers of the night, and then turn and come back toward the light, following the fire's reflection on the ice.

Later on, when some people were already making their way up the hill to the house, Eunice Lathem went skating off into the darkness with her sister. They didn't skate up the middle of the lake as most of the skaters had been doing. Instead they went off toward the east bank. There is a place there where a spring rises and the water is deep, but they didn't know that. The ice was thinner there. They broke through.

Near the fire, people heard their cries for help. A group of men skated out to rescue them. When the men got close to the place where the girls were in the water, the ice began to crack under their feet.

All the men lay down then and formed a chain, each holding the ankles of the man in front of him. Uncle Nathan was at the front. He inched forward, feeling the ice tremble beneath his body, until he came to the point where he could reach either of two pairs of hands clinging to the fractured edge.

It was dark. He couldn't see the girl's faces. All he could do was grasp the nearest pair of wrists and pull. The men behind him pulled on his feet. Together they dragged one girl back to safety. But as they were doing it the ice broke away beneath them and the second girl went under. The moon came out and they saw it was Eunice Lathem's sister they had saved. They went back to the hole, but Eunice had vanished. There wasn't any way they could even get her body.

"It was an awful thing to have happen on our place," my father said.

"Your Uncle Nathan risked his life," my mother said. Her voice was earnest, for she too believed in identifying heros and villains.

"There was no way on earth he could save both girls," she said. "The ice was already breaking, and the extra weight of the first one was bound to be too much for it."

Why hadn't he saved Eunice first?

"I told you," my mother said. "He couldn't see their faces."

It troubled me that he hadn't had some way of knowing. I would have expected love to be able to call out to love. If it couldn't do that, what was it good for? And why had the moon been behind a cloud anyway?

"Your grandmother used to say that the Lord moves in a mysterious way," my father said.

"What does that mean?" I asked.

"It means that nobody knows," my mother said.

I'd seen Eunice Lathem's name on a grave in the yard of St. Chad's, where we attended services every second Sunday. If I'd thought of her at all, it was as a person who had always been dead. Now she seemed real to me, almost like a relative. She was a girl who had loved and been loved. I began to make up stories about her. But I no longer skated on the lake alone.

Eunice Lathem's sister, whose name was Delia Sykes, moved away from Willow Bunch right after the accident. She didn't wait until her husband sold out; she went straight to Edmonton and waited for him there. Even when they buried Eunice in the spring, she didn't come back.

Years later, someone from Willow Bunch had seen her in Edmonton. She didn't mention Eunice or the accident or even Willow Bunch.

"It must have been a short conversation," my mother said practically.

Is it surprising that I continued to wonder why Uncle Nathan didn't marry? Some people remember their childhoods as a time when they thought of anybody over the age of 25 as being so decrepit as to be beyond all thought of romance or adventure. I remember feeling that way about *women*, but I never thought of men that way, whatever their ages. It seemed to me that Uncle Nathan could still pick out a girl and marry her if he set his mind to it.

"No," he said when I asked him. "Not 'still' and not 'pick out a girl.' A person doesn't have that much say in the matter. You can't love where you choose."

And then, making a joke of it, "See that you remember that when your time comes," he said.

One day my mother showed me a picture of Eunice Lathem and her sister. Two girls and a pony stood looking at the camera. Both girls were pretty. The one who wasn't Eunice was laughing; she looked like a girl who loved to laugh. Eunice was pretty too but there was a stillness about her, almost a sternness. If she hadn't been Eunice Lathem, I would have said she was sulking.

I felt cheated. Was the laughing one also prettier?

"She may have been," my mother said. "I remember Eunice Lathem as being beautiful. But since Delia Sykes was married, I don't suppose I gave her looks a thought one way or the other."

As I grew older I spent less time wondering about the girl who'd been Eunice Lathem. I'd never wondered about her sister, and perhaps never would have if I hadn't happened to be with Uncle Nathan the day he heard that Delia Sykes had died.

It was the spring I was fifteen. My parents were away for the weekend, attending a silver wedding in Rochfort Bridge. Uncle Nathan and I were alone on the farm and so, if he wanted to talk about Delia Sykes, he hadn't much choice about who to talk to.

It was a morning for bad news. The frost was coming out of the ground, setting the very ditches and wheel-ruts to weeping. Out in the barn, a ewe was mourning her lost lamb. We had put her in a pen by herself and we were saving the dead lamb, so we could use its skin to dress another lamb in case one of the ewes died in lambing or had no milk.

Uncle Nathan and I left the barn and walked out to the road to pick up the mail. The news of Delia's death was in the local paper. "Old-timers will be saddened to learn of the death in Duncan, B. C. of Mrs. Delia Sykes, a former resident of this district," the paper said.

Uncle Nathan shook his head slowly, as if he found the news hard to believe. "So Delia's gone," he said. "She was a grand girl, Delia Sykes. No matter what anybody said, she was a grand girl."

There was a picture of Mrs. Sykes with the death notice. I saw a middle-aged woman who had gone from the hairdresser's to the photographer's. Her cheeks were as firm and round as two peach halves, and she had snappy eyes. She was wearing a white dress. She looked as if she might have belonged to the Eastern Star or the Rebekahs.

Uncle Nathan looked at the picture too. "Delia always was a beauty," he said.

He sat in silence for a while, and then, bit by bit, he began to tell me the story of how he had met Delia Sykes and before her, her husband.

"Only I didn't realize that he was her husband," Uncle Nathan said. "I thought when I met her that she was single; that was the joke of it."

It was late July and late afternoon. Uncle Nathan was teaching school, to make enough money to live on until his farm got going. But he was hoping to get out of it.

"The land was new then and we thought there was no limit to how rich we were all going to be some day. Besides that," he added, "what I wanted to do was farm. School-teaching seemed to me to be no proper job for a man."

There were two things Uncle Nathan wanted. One was to stop teaching. The other was to find a wife.

There were more men than girls around then, he told me, so the man who wanted a good selection had to be prepared to cover a lot of territory.

"Harold Knight and I took in dances and ball games as far away as Hasty Hills," he said.

They'd already seen a fair sampling, but there were still girls they hadn't seen.

"I had a pretty fair idea of what I was looking for," Uncle

Nathan said. "I imagine it was the same sort of thing every young fellow thinks he's looking for, but I thought I had standards. I wasn't willing to settle for just anyone."

It was with the idea of looking over another couple of girls that he went to see Harold Knight that late July afternoon. A family with two daughters was rumoured to have moved in somewhere near Morningside School. He'd come to suggest to Harold that they take in the church service at the school the next Sunday.

The Knights, Uncle Nathan said, had hay and seed wheat to sell to people with the money to buy it. When Uncle Nathan walked into their yard that day, he saw that Mr. Knight was talking to a buyer. It was a man he'd never seen before, but he guessed by the cut of the man's rig that he must be well fixed.

"Nathan," Mr. Knight said, "meet Dobson Sykes."

Mr. Sykes was a straight-standing man with greying hair. He put out his hand and Uncle Nathan shook it.

"His driving horses," Uncle Nathan said, "were as showy a team as I'd ever seen — big bays with coats the colour of red willow."

"You'd go a long way before you'd find a better-matched team than that," Mr. Knight said.

"Oh, they match well enough." Dobson Sykes spoke as if that was a matter of little importance to him, as if no effort was made in the acquiring of such a team. "I'd trade them in a minute if something better came along," he said carelessly. "I have a job to keep Spark, here, up to his collar."

"I had a fair amount of respect then for men who'd done well in life," Uncle Nathan told me. "This man was about my father's age, old enough to have made it on his own. When a man like that came my way, I studied him. I thought if I was going to be a farmer instead of a teacher, I'd have to start figuring out how people went about getting things in life.

"I wasn't really surprised when Mr. Knight said that Sykes had a crew of men — men he was paying — putting up a set of buildings for him on a place he'd bought near Bannock Hill. He looked like a man with that kind of money."

"We're not building anything fancy," Dobson Sykes said. "If I'd wanted to stay farming on a big scale, I wouldn't have moved from Manitoba."

After a while Uncle Nathan left the two older men talking and walked out toward the meadow, where Harold was fetching a load of hay for Mr. Sykes.

It was on the trail between buildings and meadow that he met Delia Sykes.

He didn't see her at first because she wasn't sitting up front with Harold. She must have been lying back in the hay, Uncle Nathan said, just watching the clouds drift by overhead. She sat up.

Uncle Nathan saw at once that she was not very old; he had girls almost as old as she was in his classroom. But there was nothing of the schoolgirl about Delia. She was young but womanly. Everything about her curved, from the line of her cheek to the way she carried her arms.

Uncle Nathan saw all this in the instant that she appeared looking down over the edge of the load. He saw too that she had a kind of class he'd never seen around Willow Bunch. She looked like a girl perfectly suited to riding around the country behind a team of perfectly matched bays.

She reached behind her into the hay and came up with a crown of french-braided dandelions. She set it on top of her hair and smiled.

He knew right then, Uncle Nathan said, that his voice wouldn't be among those swelling the hymns at Morningside School next Sunday. And he felt as if he understood for the first time how men must feel when they are called to the ministry. Choosing and decision and standards have nothing to do with it.

You're called or you're not called, and when you're called you know it.

The girl smiled and opened her arms as if to take in the clouds in the sky and the bees buzzing in the air and the red-topped grasses stirring in the wind. Then she spoke.

"You've got no worries on a load of hay," she said.

Those were the first words Uncle Nathan heard Delia Sykes say. "You've got no worries on a load of hay."

There was a patch of milkweed blooming near the path where Uncle Nathan was standing. In late July, small pink blossoms appear and the milk, rich and white, is ready to run as soon as you break the stalk. Uncle Nathan picked a branch, climbed the load of hay, and presented it to the girl.

"It's not roses," he said, "but the sap is supposed to cure warts."

She laughed. "My name is Delia Sykes," she said.

"I thought she was Dobson's daughter," Uncle Nathan said, "and it crossed my mind to wonder if he'd have traded her off if she hadn't moved along smart in her harness.

"There didn't seem much fear of that. You could see right away she had a spirit. If she had too much, it was nothing that marriage to a good man wouldn't cure, I thought."

Uncle Nathan gave a rueful smile. "Of course when we got back to the yard I found out that she wasn't Dobson's daughter but his wife. Later I wondered why she hadn't introduced herself as Mrs. Sykes. And she'd called me *Nathan* too, and girls didn't do that then.

"The truth is," Uncle Nathan said, "I had kind of fallen for her."

Did she feel the same way about him?

If she did, Uncle Nathan wasn't willing to say so. "Delia was only nineteen," he said. "I don't think she knew what she wanted."

He was silent for a while. Then he went on with his story. "Once I knew she was married," he said, "I knew right away what I had to do. I remember I gave myself a good talking to.

I said, 'If you can fall in love in twenty minutes, you can fall out of love just as fast.' "

"And could you?"

"Some people could, I guess," Uncle Nathan said. "It seemed to take me a bit longer than that."

The story stopped then because we had to go out to the barn to check the sheep. While we'd been in the house, another ewe had dropped her lamb. We heard it bleat as we came in the barn, and the ewe whose lamb had died heard it too. It was at the far end of the barn, out of sight, but at the sound of it, milk began to run from her udder. She couldn't help herself.

We checked the rest of the sheep and then we went back into the house. I made us a pot of tea.

"I was afraid to go to see Dobson and Delia after they got moved in," Uncle Nathan said. "I think I was afraid somebody would read my mind."

He went, he said, because Delia soon made her house a gathering place for all the young people of the district, and he didn't see how he could be the only one to stay away. Delia didn't make things any easier for him.

"She used to keep saying she'd only been married three months . . . as if that made it any less final. And when she spoke of anything they had — whether it was a buggy or a kitchen safe or the pet dog — she would say 'my buggy' or 'my kitchen safe' or 'my dog'. 'We' and 'us' were words she didn't use at all."

I poured our tea then, trying to imagine the house that Delia Sykes had lived in.

"It was something of a showplace for its time," Uncle Nathan told me. Everything in it was the best of its kind, he said, from the Home Comfort stove in the kitchen to the pump organ in the parlour. What puzzled Uncle Nathan was Delia's attitude to her things. She'd picked them out herself in Winnipeg and ordered them sent, but when they got here, she seemed to feel they weren't important.

212   Man *vs* Himself

"The more things you've got, the more things you've got to take care of," she said. She didn't even unpack most of her trunks.

Dobson was worried. He thought that moving away from her family had unsettled her. "Delia wasn't like this in Manitoba," he said.

"I kept wondering," Uncle Nathan said, "where we would go from here. It never occurred to me that there could be another girl for me. And then Eunice came along."

It was on an October afternoon, Uncle Nathan said, that he met Eunice Lathem.

The sun was low in the southwest when he drove into the Sykes yard, and Dobson, as usual, was out around the buildings showing the younger men his grinding mill, his blacksmith shop, his threshing machine.

Uncle Nathan remembered that the trees were leafless except for the plumes of new growth at the top. He tied up his horse and, as he headed for the house, saw that the afternoon sun was turning the west-facing walls all gold and blue. It looked like a day for endings, not beginnings. But he went into the house, and there stood Eunice Lathem.

Eunice was a year or two older than Delia but she looked just like her. Uncle Nathan noticed that she was quieter.

Supper was already on the table when Uncle Nathan got there. The news of Eunice's arrival had attracted such a company of bachelors that there weren't enough plates or chairs for everybody to eat at once.

"I don't know about anybody else, but I'm starving," Delia announced, taking her place at the head of the table. Eunice, though she was the guest of honour, insisted on waiting until the second sitting.

As the first eaters prepared to deal with their pie, Eunice began to ladle water out of the stoneware crock into a dishpan. Uncle Nathan went to help her. He said something funny and she laughed.

Delia's voice startled them both. "I invited Eunice out here to find a husband," she said with a high-pitched laugh. "I said to myself, 'With all the bachelors we've got around, if she can't find a husband here, there's no hope for her.'"

Delia spoke as if she were making a joke, and there was a nervous round of laughter. Blood rose in Eunice's face.

"If I'd known that was why you were asking me," Eunice said, "I would never have come."

And indeed, Uncle Nathan said, Eunice wasn't the sort of girl to need anyone's help in finding a husband. She was, if anything, prettier than Delia. Not as showy, perhaps, perhaps not as rounded. But if you went over them point by point comparing noses, chins, teeth and all the rest of it, Eunice might well have come out on top.

Later, when the others had gone, Delia apologized. "I shouldn't have said that," she said. "It sounded awful." She didn't even claim to have been making a joke.

"I want you two to be friends," she said.

In the weeks that followed, Uncle Nathan saw that Delia was pushing her sister his way. He didn't know why, but he didn't find the idea unpleasant.

"I suppose I liked Eunice at first because she looked so much like Delia," he said, "but as I got to know her better it seemed to me that she might be easier to get along with in the long run. I wouldn't be the first man to marry the sister of the girl who first took his fancy, nor the last one either.

"It seemed to me that a man could love one girl as easily as another if he put his mind to it. I reasoned it out. How much did the person matter anyway? That was what I asked myself. It seemed to me that when all was said and done, it would be the life that two people made together that would count, not who the people were.

"I remember thinking that getting married would be like learning to dance. Some people are born knowing how; they have a natural beat. Other people have to make an effort to learn. But all of them, finally, are moving along to the music one way or the other.

"Anyway," Uncle Nathan said, "I spoke to Eunice, and she agreed, and we decided to be married at Christmas.

"It was September, I think, when we got engaged," Uncle Nathan said. "I remember thinking about telling Dobson and Delia. I could imagine the four of us — Dobson and Delia, Eunice and me — living side by side, spending our Sundays together, raising children who would be cousins and might even look like each other.

"I came over early on the Sunday and we told them. Delia didn't have very much to say then. But in the afternoon when quite a crowd had gathered and Eunice and I were waiting for the rest of them to get there before we made our announcement, a strange thing happened.

"The day before, Dobson had brought home a new saddle pony and Delia had wanted to ride it. Dobson didn't know how well broke it was, or if it could be trusted, and he refused. I guess that refusal rankled. Delia didn't like to be told she couldn't do a thing or have a thing she had set her heart on.

"Anyway, on Sunday afternoon Eunice was sitting at the pump organ playing for us, and she looked beautiful. We were all sitting around looking at her. "And then somebody happened to glance out of the window," Uncle Nathan said. "And there was Delia on the pony, and the pair of them putting on a regular rodeo.

"She didn't break her neck, which was a wonder. By the time she finally got off the pony, we were all out in the yard, and somebody had the idea of taking a picture of Delia and Eunice and the pony."

After that, Uncle Nathan said, Delia seemed to want to get the wedding over with as soon as possible. She hemmed sheets and ordered linen and initialled pillow-cases. When November finally came and the neighbours decided on a skating party for Eunice and Uncle Nathan, it was Delia who sewed white rabbit fur around the sleeves and bottom of Eunice's coat, so that it would look like a skating dress.

The night of the party was dark. There was a moon, but the sky was cloudy. They walked down the hill together, all those young people, laughing and talking.

"One minute you could see their faces and the next they would all disappear," Uncle Nathan said. "I touched a match to a bonfire we had laid in the afternoon, and we all sat down to screw on our skates.

"I skated first with Eunice. She wanted to stay near the fire so we could see where we were going. I skated with several other girls, putting off, for some reason, the time when I would skate with Delia. But then she came gliding up to me and held out her hands, and I took them and we headed out together into the darkness.

"As soon as we turned our backs on the fire it was as if something came over us. We wanted to skate out farther and farther. It seemed to me that we could keep on like this all our lives, just skating outward farther and farther, and the lake would keep getting longer and longer so that we would never come to the end of it."

Uncle Nathan sighed. "I didn't know then that in three days Delia would have left Willow Bunch for good, and in six months I would have followed her," he said.

Why had he given up farming?

"Farming's no life for a man alone," he said. "And I couldn't imagine ever wanting to marry again."

He resumed his story. "Once the moon came out and I could see Delia's face, determined in the moonlight.

" 'Do you want to turn back?' I asked her.

" 'I'm game as long as you are,' she said.

"Another time, 'I don't ever want to turn back,' she said.

"I gave in before Delia did," Uncle Nathan said.

" 'If we don't turn around pretty soon,' I told her, 'we're going to be skating straight up Pa's stubble fields.'

"We turned around then, and there was the light from the fire and our feet already set on its path. And I found I wanted to be back there with all the people around me. Eunice deserved better, and I knew it."

As they came toward the fire, Eunice skated out to meet them. "I might as well have been someplace else for all the attention she paid me," Uncle Nathan said. "Her words were all for Delia."

"If this is what you got me out here for," Eunice said, "you can just forget about it. I'm not going to be your window blind."

"I don't know what you're talking about," Delia said.

She looked unhappy. "She knew as well as I did," Uncle Nathan said, "that whatever we were doing out there, it was more than just skating."

"We were only skating," Delia said. And then her temper rose. "You always were jealous of me," she said.

"Who would you say was jealous now?" Eunice asked.

"We were far enough away from the fire for the girls not to be heard," Uncle Nathan said. "At least I hoped we were.

"What was worrying me was the thought of Eunice having to meet all the people at the house, and finding out she was the guest of honour, and having to try to rise to the occasion.

"That was why I suggested that the two of them go for a skate. I thought it would give them a chance to cool down. Besides," he added, "I couldn't think of anything else to do."

The girls let themselves be persuaded. They skated off together and Uncle Nathan watched them go. First he could see their two silhouettes, slim and graceful against the silver lake. Then all he could see was the white fur on Eunice's coat. And then they were swallowed up by the darkness.

"It was several minutes before we heard them calling for help," Uncle Nathan said.

Uncle Nathan and I sat silent for some time then: he remembering, I pondering. "If only you could have seen how beautiful she was," he said at last, and I didn't know whether it was Eunice he was speaking of, or Delia.

"I wonder if I would have felt any better about it if I'd got Eunice instead of Delia," he said. I realized that he'd been trying to make the judgement for 30 years.

"You didn't have any choice," I reminded him. "It was dark. You couldn't see their faces."

"No," Uncle Nathan said. "I couldn't see their faces." The sound of old winters was in his voice, a sound of infinite sadness.

"But I could see their hands on the edge of the ice," he said. "The one pair of arms had white fur around them.

"And I reached for the other pair."

"Merry Christmas, Doctor!"
Leslie J. Olson

Dark figures advanced carefully to the edge of the wooded area; their frosted breaths, a white mist in the moonlight. Snow swished as their boots methodically rose and fell. Moonlight glinted off rifle barrels. They crouched down near a white crowned bush, whispering in soft tones.

"What do you think, Paul?" their leader queried, rubbing his nose with a gloved hand.

"Looks quiet enough," came the reply, "but I don't like it. It's too quiet."

The Sergeant nodded, "I know what you mean, I've got that feeling too."

Motioning the other three men up, he half whispered, "We'll dodge around this clearing, and scout the other side. If any of you get separated from the rest, we'll meet here in one hour. Remember, no noise. This place may be crawling with Germans. Any questions?"

The helmeted men shook their heads, nervously glancing off into the darkness.

"Let's go then," continued Burkdale, getting to his feet.

The five soldiers circled warily around the clearing. Paul felt cold; colder than he'd been since they'd pushed into Germany.

His whiskered face tingled from the frost and his forehead became numb. The temperature was falling rapidly. Paul was glad to know they would be turning back soon; back to camp where they had a warm fire, and sheltered fox holes. Tomorrow was Christmas, but it seemed odd to him. Christmas was a Christmas tree, an open fire in the hearth, and a turkey dinner on the table. Not a cold foxhole with a tin of half-frozen K-rations.

Another halt was called, and he went forward to converse with Sergeant Burkdale.

"I guess the Nazis are keeping still tonight. We may as well report back to our outfit. Okay with you, Norton?"

Paul nodded, too cold to speak.

"Okay, boys, we'll head back," mumbled Burkdale through stiff jaws.

Paul kneeled in the snow to retrieve the glove he had dropped.

Flashes suddenly spurted from the trees to their right. Hot steel screamed by, as a machine gun stuttered its death chant. Instinctively throwing himself flat, Norton swung his Bren Gun around, released the safety, then squeezed off a long burst.

"We sure walked into this trap with our eyes closed," Paul muttered to himself, snapping another clip to his weapon.

The sergeant had caught the first volley, which had almost cleaved his body in half. Of the other three, two were sprawled out in the snow, and the third was slowly crawling back towards Paul, leaving dark splotches behind. Emptying his Bren Gun a second time, Paul Norton reached out and pulled the wounded soldier behind the log where he was lying. It was Glen Daniels, a university student from Edmonton.

Daniels sobbed through clenched teeth, "Help me Paul, stop the pain, I can't stand it!"

Paul glanced at the soldier's stomach. Blood oozed out in a steady flow. The boy was dying. He injected a shot of morphine, then said reassuringly, "Hold on boy, you'll be okay. I'll have you out of here and back before you know it. The medic will fix you up good as new."

"Thanks Paul, I hope . . ." he faltered.

Norton checked for pulse. Daniels was dead.

With a bitter taste in his mouth, Paul lay the boy back. He was alone now, alone and scared.

The firing had stopped. No sound broke the stillness of the night, no movement showed the presence of his attackers. Four bodies lay grotesquely sprawled in the snow, four bodies of four close friends. Voices came from the direction of the firing, crisp and clear in the cold. The Germans thought he was dead! Paul waited, his Bren Gun was trained on the sounds. Four Germans stepped cautiously out into the small opening, still uncertain of their success in the ambush. One, laughing loudly, kicked at the Sergeant's body. Cold anger mounted, as Paul's finger tightened on the trigger.

"Laugh at this, you lousy Butchers," he screamed, holding the trigger back. Taken by surprise, the four Germans were chopped down by the first blast of steel.

Warily, watching for any movement, Norton rose from behind his shelter. The acid smell of gunpowder stung his nose. Poking the first body with his boot, Paul turned the German over. There was no life in the first. The slugs had caught the soldier dead centre. Moving on to the next, he kicked out with his boot. To his astonishment, the enemy soldier rolled over, bringing up a Luger! The Bren Gun chattered viciously. Something smashed into his head. Then blackness flared, enveloping him with merciful arms.

A bright star grew in the blackness. It grew larger, dissipating the darkness; bringing on sudden pain. He blinked his eyes, smarting from the brightness. Where was he? The German with the Luger! With a start he tried to sit up. Sudden pain made him gasp, and fall back.

"Easy, Comrade," a heavily accented voice cautioned. "You've got a nasty wound on your head. An inch deeper your brains would be splattered all over your helmet."

Paul started, then reached for a rifle that lay nearby.

"Take it easy Comrade, I will not harm you," the German soldier repeated, pulling the rifle away.

Paul blinked, then studied the man with questioning eyes.

"I'm a medic," the soldier continued, "I found you with a mass of corpses and if you hadn't moved, I would have passed you by. I dressed your wound and I've got some hot soup on. Want some?"

Paul nodded, still too dizzy to speak. The soup was thin and watery, but it was hot. Then glancing around, he surveyed his position. They seemed to be under the limbs of a large tree. The ground there was bare, now partially covered with the soiled blanket he was lying on. A small fire could be seen burning through an opening in the branches. A makeshift soup kettle was propped up over the flames, which was fed by a few small limbs. He noted that the fire was smokeless.

The German followed his glances and smiled, "I didn't want to be interrupted by any friends of yours, or mine either!" he added with emphasis.

That made sense to Paul. A German soldier, caught helping an enemy, was shot on the spot. It would be just as fatal to be caught by the other side, because neither side was taking prisoners.

"What were you doing out here alone?" Paul questioned, suddenly suspicious. "Were you with the others?" he asked again, he eyes suddenly steel cold.

"Look here Corporal, had I been with them, you would be

lying out there now, and not in here with me. I don't want to know what happened out there. We're enemies, and it was my duty to finish you off. I didn't because I'm a doctor and I swore to save lives, not take them. The answer to your first question is simple. My outfit pulled back and I got separated from the rest in the confusion. I was trying to find my way when I heard the commotion. When I arrived, all I found was a number of very dead soldiers, or so I thought until you moved. I carried you over here and doctored your head. I guess that's it." He made a motion towards the soup. "Want some more?"

Paul nodded his head. His mess tin was again filled, this time with the last of the broth. The warmth of the soup was beginning to thaw Paul out. His head ached dully, but the dizziness had disappeared.

"You speak good English."

"Yes, I studied medicine in London before the war."

"How did you get into Hitler's hands?"

"I came back here for a visit and the Gestapo nabbed me. They needed doctors. I didn't have much to say in the matter, so here I am." The doctor shrugged his shoulders resignedly.

"Why don't you get out?"

"You mean desert? Maybe I will, but it doesn't really matter. I can save lives here as well as anywhere else."

"What about your life? You would be shot now if you were caught helping me."

The doctor shrugged his shoulders. "What's the difference, I have nothing to live for."

"Haven't you a family; maybe a girl or a wife in Berlin, or wherever you came from?"

Avoiding Paul's eyes, the doctor replied, "I had a girl once. She was killed during a bombing raid in Berlin."

"I'm sorry, I shouldn't have asked," Paul apologized.

"No need to; I've accepted it and lived with it for nearly three years."

A rumble of artillery echoed through the forest. The doctor

turned towards the rumble, estimating the nearness of the action. Paul noticed a livid scar running from the doctor's temple to his chin. Probably a recent bayonet wound.

The sounds neared. Nervously the German doctor gathered his pack. "I'd better move on, before your friends arrive." He motioned towards the rumbling.

"Well soldier, good luck."

"Thanks."

Hesitating, the doctor smiled. "Merry Christmas," he added, then was gone.

Paul realized he'd forgotten that it was Christmas! He could thank the doctor for being alive for Christmas.

Thirty minutes later he was reporting to his commanding officer. After making a detailed report, he was ordered back to the base hospital for a rest. He'd done his share. Now he could get away from the killing; the wounded; and the dying. A machine gun rattled somewhere ahead of the advancing soldiers. Drawn back by an uneasy feeling, Paul followed another soldier to the source of the sound. A few yards further they spotted a uniformed man kneeling beside two figures in the snow. The kneeling soldier rose as he came up.

"He was bending over one of our scouts. I thought he was a sniper and had shot one of our boys. I guess he was only trying to help the wounded man."

Examining the body, Paul stared at the face. A livid scar ran up one side of the face.

Paul could utter only three words. "Merry Christmas, doctor."

Acknowledgements

The editor wishes to thank the authors and publishers for permission to include the following in this anthology:

Beacon Press for "Survival" by Eugene S. Hollman from *Ways of Mankind.*

The Canadian Publishers, McClelland and Stewart Limited for "Prairie Fire at Gully Farm" by Mary Hiemstra from *Gully Farm.*

Colleen DeJong for "The Trapper" from *Reflections of Moments Literary Magazine,* Bowness Composite High School, Bowness, Alberta.

Doubleday Canada Limited for "The Fire" by Eric Nicol from *Vancouver.*

Ted Ferguson for "The Last Great Train Robbery" from *Golden West.*

Frontier Publishing Ltd. for "Brother, It's Hot!" by Frank W. Anderson from *Regina's Terrible Tornado.*

Gage Publishing Limited for "Jimmy Was No Hero" by Marion Brooker. For "Watch the Fires Burn" by Samuel Roddan from *Rubaboo* (1962).

Robert E. Gard for "Avalanche".

Gray's Publishing Limited for "The Barber of Barkerville" by Cecil Clark from *Tales of the British Columbia Provincial Police.*

Macmillan Company of Canada Ltd. for "Harvester Patrol" by T. Morris Longstreth from *In Scarlet and Plain Clothes.* For "On Being Lost" by Grey Owl from *The Men of the Last Frontier.*

McGraw-Hill Ryerson Limited for "The Spell of the Yukon" by Robert W. Service from *The Collected Poems of Robert Service.*

Oberon Press for "The Skating Party" by Merna Summers from *The Skating Party.*

Frank Walker for "Red River Rising" from *The Beaver.*

Western Producer Prairie Books for "The Bootlegger" by A. L. Freebairn from *Wake the Prairie Echoes: The Story of the R.C.M.P. in Verse,* collected by the Saskatchewan Folklore and History Society.

Jon Whyte for "The Agony of Mrs. Stone".

While every effort has been made to trace the owners of copyrighted material and to make due acknowledgment, we regret having been unsuccessful with the following selections:

"Disaster At Avalanche Mountain" by Cecil Clark.

"Mercy Flight" by Armour MacKay from *The Beaver.*

"Merry Christmas, Doctor!" by Leslie J. Olson from *Centennial Leaf.*

"Ladysmith's Death Watch" by T. W. Paterson.

"The Working Man" by Kim Pirie.

"At Grips with a Grizzly" by Colin Wyatt from *Maclean's.*